ADVANCE PRAISE

"As an avid traveling motorcyclist, my video recorder was set to record American Thunder to watch the show's host, Michele Smith, travel and report from the motorcycle rallies of Sturgis and Daytona. Michele is a savvy entrepreneur and passionate traveler. I call her my 'Gypsy MC friend' because of her constant travel to exotic places. I will live vicariously through Michele's adventures abroad."

—MICHAEL W. O'NEILL, ESQ., GENERAL COUNSEL

"I love traveling with this girl. She keeps everyone regaled with fun and crazy stories. Michele even made me forget that we were actually hiking for miles a day on the Camino. We managed to have a magical and spiritual trip and I attribute that mostly to her. A fascinating and fun read from my longtime friend."

—LORI EISENBERG, PROPERTY DEVELOPER, LOS ANGELES

"Michele Smith is a dear friend whom I have known forever through our work in the entertainment industry. I thought I knew everything about Michele, but after reading her memoir, boy was I wrong! She has always lived life to its fullest, and now I understand why. I love her even more after reading about her life's adventures and wisdom in this inspiring and a bit shocking tell-all book!"

—WILLIAM SQUIRE, OWNER, BILLY'S BLUES COSMETICS
AND YOUR SIGNATURE STYLE EVENTS

"Not every kid gets to grow up with a model, TV host, and world-traveling aunt—but I did! My Aunt Michele was the epitome of cool in our family, and still is. She was living the 'you only live once' lifestyle long before it was a saying, living life relentlessly and without giving a damn about what anyone else thought! I'm glad the rest of the world can finally get a taste of her zest for life and rock-star attitude!"

—RACHAEL MICHELE PENTON, AWARD-WINNING CHIEF METEOROLOGIST, KALB-TV

"About fifteen years ago I was in Palm Beach, looking for a model to photograph for my clothing designs. I arranged to interview a potential candidate and was awestruck when I met Michele. Not only is she beautiful, intelligent, and kind, her personality exemplifies grace and gratitude. Over the years we've exchanged stories of our travels and the wonderful experiences we both have in common. Her travels and wonderful memoir have influenced my creativity. 38 is a great read."

—DEAN ALAN, DESIGNER AND OWNER, DEAN ALAN LIFESTYLE

"I met Michele when she came into my salon. As her hairstylist I listened and lived vicariously through her many exciting stories! Her parties were always fabulous...I even worked for her when she had her sexy edible panty line! Lots of laughs and great memories! She is a great friend."

—CHLOE HOLGUIN, HOLLYWOOD CELEBRITY STYLIST, CHAZ DEAN STUDIO

"I first met Michele twelve years ago at a motorcycle show in Atlantic City that my friend and I attended. I recognized her and said, 'Hey, that's that girl Michele Smith who hosts American Thunder on the Speed Channel.' Happily, we got to meet her, and she was *so nice and friendly, and funny too. Through the years I have seen her at many different MC shows, and she has always been friendly, remembered me, and teased me about previous conversations. I'm happy that she is enjoying her life and traveling around the world."*

—DAVE JAMES, FAN, FRIEND, AND CAN-AM SPYDER RIDER

"From my earliest memories with my Aunt Michele, she was living life to the fullest. Traveling the world, having endless stories filled with adventure, glamor, and humor. Her carefree personality will motivate you to make the most of the time you have. I am excited that the rest of the world gets a deeper dive into who she is and know they will feel inspired to live life in fast-forward too!"

—KATIE PENTON, PRINCIPAL CONSULTANT, INTELLETEC

"Who knew that all my prodigious years spent with Michele would end up in a book! We had Love, Laughs, and Lust. It was quite a time for both of us. Through our travels I gave her a taste of the good life and caused her to have an unquenchable thirst for more. Reading this book took me back to memory lane!"

—"THE DUTCHMAN"

"I can't remember what motorcycle show I first met Michele at—it has to be at least fifteen years ago. I stopped in to say hi and introduce myself. Michele's charm and charisma sucked me in, and even though we seem like total opposites, we became fast friends and have been ever since. After that I would always search her out at events. We would chat and catch up, talk about new products or how the show was. We realized how many mutual friends we had and that led to many dinners and drinks with everyone after the events. The amount of laughs and jokes we've had over the years is too many to list. It also helps that she's a very easy girl to make laugh. With her magnetic charm and personality, dinners or drinks were quite memorable. I

truly miss seeing her at the events—it was always a highlight of that show. Her book captures her personality and also tells a great story of adventure and living life to its fullest! Love that girl!"

—DOUG ASERMELY, OWNER, SICK BOY MOTORCYCLES

"What a lady, what a life, what a book! Getting to know Michele through her life stories has been a privilege and joy. She's complex, caring, compassionate, funny as hell, irreverent, and deeply spiritual. In other words, a whole woman. I highly recommend you read 38: Traveling My Life in Fast-Forward to be inspired, challenged out of your complacency, and called to hit the road. You'll be glad you did."

—LAURA BOULAY, WORDSMITH,
GHOSTWRITER, BRAND CONSULTANT

"I have been shooting this girl since 1989, way before digital was a thing—if you can believe that one! And we always manage to get amazing photos. She's still doing it and she always has a story to tell from her travels. Good to know it's finally all in a book! Love the read!"

—MARCEL INDIK, LOS ANGELES FASHION PHOTOGRAPHER

"The average person spends most of their life working and waiting for the day they retire so they can really start 'living.' Michele doesn't put off living until the perfect time. She lives every day to the fullest, always looking for life's next adventure. I've been fortunate to experience some of these adventures with her—attending motorcycle events throughout the Northeast, cruising throughout the Western Caribbean, zip coastering in Costa Rica, dancing at La Guérite Restaurant Cannes, and most recently, climbing a bell tower in the medieval village of Saint-Émilion. Our dad often said there was only one Michele, that the mold had been broken with her. He was right, there truly is no one else like her. She is the most generous person that I know, she is protective of those she loves, she

is strong, and fiercely independent. Michele dances to the beat of her own drum, she enjoys life, and she encourages others to do the same. Enjoy reading Michele's travel memoirs and be inspired to find your next adventure."

—LISA SPONG, DIRECTOR OF ADMINISTRATION, STORABLE

"I met Michele in 1995 at a friend's birthday party in Beverly Hills. If I had to write everything about us, it would be a novel! She became my best friend, part of my family, and my one true love. She was an angel to me when I was fighting with my own demons. I owe her more than words can say. She is a unique soul—kind, caring, and generous, beautiful inside and out. She will be in my heart to the end, and I will always be there for her as I know she will be there for me. Her book is a wonderful read, a mixture of adventure, travel, and so many unique personalities. It's as beautiful as its author!"

—FREDDY KESHMIRI, BEVERLY HILLS JEWELER

"I have known Michele for almost seven years now. I love the fact that she is a very open and honest person who has lived a fabulous life. Listening to her stories makes me laugh and sometimes even gasp. She is a lover of life and travel and has visited some of the most extraordinary places. She is an inspiration to me as a fellow entrepreneur. I want to be her when I grow up! Reading the book was such a delight!"

—EDYE MARCHESE, OWNER, BELLA SKIN EXPERTS

"I met Michele when she first came to LA, at one of those bikini contests she mentions. I was a photographer scouting for bikini calendar models, and she was perfect. We worked together often and are still great friends. Her life is always an adventure. She's certainly one of a kind."

—ANDY PEARLMAN, RETIRED HOLLYWOOD
PINUP PHOTOGRAPHER

"My mother introduced me to Michele when she came into our store in Mykonos. I was her Greek God. Soon I was visiting her in LA with trips to Vegas and Florida. She gave me the chance to see the States. I then invited her to Thailand, and next thing you know I found myself riding an elephant with her. She's had so many amazing adventures, and I'm so happy she finally put them all into a book. You're going to love it!"

—STATHIS KONTARINIS, THE CORNER
JEWELRY STORE, MYKONOS

"I have worked with Michele often over the last twenty years, and we always create magic in our sessions! Not only is Michele beautiful on the outside, she is beautiful on the inside!"

—JON ABEYTA, CELEBRITY PHOTOGRAPHER, LOS ANGELES

"Michele is my younger sister. She is one of a kind—beautiful, and oh so funny! We have always been close and talk daily. Some days, I'll pick up the phone and she is just laughing, hysterically, which then gets me laughing hysterically. She's the only one that I can do this with. There is always some crazy story to follow, and I mean crazy! Michele is generous and would give you the shirt off her back, even if it's Chanel! She's traveled the world, she's carefree and never worries about anything in life. I've always told her she should write a book. I hope you enjoy this great read."

—CINDY SMITH PENTON, DOMESTIC ENGINEER

"As all the sages in history have said, 'It's about the journey. A journey in pursuit of happiness.' If I were to take one person on this journey to entertain and live the Dolce Vita, it would be Michele. This book takes you on an exquisite journey, full of new discoveries and self-growth."

—WSN

38

38

TRAVELING MY LIFE IN FAST-FORWARD

MICHELE SMITH

38

Traveling My Life in Fast-Forward

FIRST EDITION

ISBN   978-1-5445-3890-7   *Hardcover*
       978-1-5445-3891-4   *Paperback*
       978-1-5445-3892-1   *Ebook*

Contents

Thank You

THIS BOOK HAPPENED BECAUSE OF THE COLLABORATION OF two people. First, I'm grateful to my longtime friend and makeup artist/stylist William Squire, whose words of encouragement got me started. Without him, quite honestly, this book would have never been written. Second, during the pandemic I reconnected with Laura Boulay, an old acquaintance who became my editor, wordsmith, project manager, and sometimes even therapist! She has been there for me every step of the way, guiding me and teaching me everything I need to know about the writing process and so much more.

Thank you, William and Laura, for helping me to figure out this next phase of my life! Without the two of you, I would still be sitting on my ass thinking about how to get started.

Thank you to my family:

To my dad who did everything for us until we began our own paths in life.

To my stepmother who did the best she could at being merged into a ready-made family.

To my sister Cindy, who for many years said, "You should keep a diary to remember all your stories. You should write a book!" I always said diaries are dangerous, but here it is—finally, a book!

To my brother Randy—read, laugh, and enjoy!

To my little sister Lisa—time passes us by quickly. Now is your time to live your best life; get out and see the world!

And to all of my nephews and nieces, this is for you, because I have no kids to call my own. It's up to you to make your own paths in life—travel, love, share, be kind, and create wonderful stories with beautiful people from all over the world so one day you can write your own books and live one hell of a fabulous life!

Thank you to all of my friends around the world who have listened to my stories over the years and kept asking when the book was coming—here it is!

To my Dutchman, *Ik houd van je tot het einde*. Without you, my life would have been so much less and so would my stories. Thank you.

A very special thanks to JS for helping me to get started on this journey.

And to MS, thank you for allowing me to finish my journey.

I am grateful.

Preface

I'VE ALWAYS FELT THAT MY TIME WAS SHORT ON THIS EARTH. I was convinced I would be dead by the age of thirty-eight. After all, that's the age my mother was when she passed.

So for many years I lived my life in fast-forward...

PART I

PA to LA

So You Know…

1 LOST TWO VERY IMPORTANT FEMALE FIGURES IN MY LIFE when I was young—my mother when I was six, and my grandmother when I was twelve. When my mom died, at least I had my grandmother, but then she left us as well. These losses undeniably impacted my life.

As a young girl, you want encouragement and advice from your mother or grandmother. You want to be able to sit down and have a conversation with your mother; you want her to be there for your birthdays and holidays, and you want her to teach you about life itself.

When your life keeps skipping a page you wonder, *where will I end up?* Some people can't seem to let go of the fact that they lost someone important in their life, but it actually made me stronger. I also have a hard outside shell that is difficult to crack—but it's getting easier with age.

There has always been a void in my life. It took years for me to figure out that the void is probably from losing my mother so young.

Me at three! Christmas 1965.

THOSE FUCKING ASHTRAYS

And so my life went on. I think at some point every one of my elementary school teachers must have looked at me as *the girl without a mother.* Or at least it seemed that way. I'll never forget our weekly art teacher. Every year for Mother's Day, my classmates and I had to make a gift for our mothers. It was always the same art project and the same teacher.

We had to make ashtrays from clay and then paint them. It was the '70s—I guess the school assumed all mothers smoked in the '70s. *Imagine if kids had to make ashtrays today! Parents would send letters and file lawsuits!*

And every year, that art teacher would walk up to my desk, lean over me, and ask, "Who will you be making your ashtray for?"

I could feel the entire class looking at me and thinking, *Oh, that girl without a mom.* And every year, I would say it was for my dad or my grandma. It felt like she asked me the question about that fucking ashtray a million times, until finally one year she asked, and I said, "I will be giving it to my stepmother!" I could have said a few other choice words, which I'm sure would have gotten me a good paddle—again, the '70s.

After that, the little old lady never asked me again, and I was so happy to leave elementary school and those fucking ashtrays behind.

THE PATH CHANGES...AGAIN

About six years after my mom died, my paternal grandmother passed away. My siblings and I called her "Mom" or "Mom Smith." To this day, I'm not really sure why—maybe we heard our dad call her "Mom," and we didn't have a mom of our own anymore.

Her death affected me more than the passing of my own mother because I knew my grandmother longer. I was twelve when she died. She was the one who helped take care of us after our mom passed or if my dad had to go out of town.

I still remember exactly where I was when I found out. I was sitting in the doctor's office, waiting to get some kind of immunization for school. My dad walked in and told me, and I burst out crying. We saved the immunization for a later date and left the office. Her death seemed more shocking because I understood it a little bit better.

Again, in the face of great loss, my life probably skipped a page, and I took a road I wouldn't have otherwise. I think with each major event in my life, the path I was originally intended for changed.

By the time my grandmother passed away, my dad was remarried, and I had a stepmother. I'm not going to say it was easy having this new woman in the house, but then again, I don't think It was easy for her, either. She came into our lives in her mid-thirties, having never been married before. Marrying my widowed dad was a package deal: three kids included.

I was ten when they married. It was great in the beginning, but that quickly changed. I remember how I hated being told what to do or what I could and could not wear to school. And sometimes it turned into a battle. *No jeans to school, huh?* I would hide the pants in my bag and change at a friend's house along the way. Then I would change again on my way home.

I think back to the time she put braids in my hair on school picture day. This was one of the few days I actually walked to school on my own. I'm glad I did, because halfway to school, right before reaching the crossing guard, I dropped my school books on the ground and ripped those ugly braids out of my hair!

I figured she would never know...well, at least not until the school pictures came back a few months later. Then she asked, "What happened to your nice braids?" I said, "I took them out because I didn't like them." And to this day, I love that school photo!

Now, I wasn't such a pleasant kid in my teenage years. Actually, I was kind of bad. In junior high, I smoked pot in the alley before school with the rest of the kids. And I did the same on Wednesday nights before catechism.

One day, my friends and I decided to skip a few classes and leave early. We ran off the school grounds and stopped at the local mini-mart to grab some snacks. We were standing by the ice cream case at the back of the store, our bikes parked in front, when here she comes—my stepmother! What could we do?! We were busted for sure, or so we thought.

A friend and I quickly bent over that ice cream case and dropped our heads deep into the freezer like two ostriches, and held that position until she left the store. Lucky for us, she wasn't buying any ice cream that day. She was buying cigarettes, probably so she could use one of those fucking ashtrays I had to make in elementary school!

THREE MILE ISLAND

In 1979, when I was a junior in high school, our local nuclear power plant, Three Mile Island, experienced a meltdown. I'm sure you've heard of it—just so happens to have been one of the most significant events in the history of US power plants.

I didn't even really know what nuclear power was—I was so clueless. I guess we never thought much about living so close to the nuclear reactors along the Susquehanna River. In fact, our house had a clear view of the reactors in the winter when the leaves had fallen from the trees.

After the meltdown, it seemed like every two minutes, the school loudspeaker would call out a student's name to come to the office. Parents were pulling their kids out of school so they could leave the area. People were panicked and not exactly sure what was happening with the leaking radiation.

We were told to stay inside.

Keep in mind, the movie *The China Syndrome*, which depicts a fictional nuclear meltdown, had been released in mid-March 1979. Less than two weeks later, the Three Mile Island accident occurred, so people were paranoid.

My dad didn't know what to do. I think he was getting mixed messages from the news. He must have been nervous, though, because we did end up leaving. I asked him what would happen if the plant blew up, and he said we wouldn't be able to return. That was hard to grasp as a teenager a year away from graduating. I remember thinking, *Where do you end up if something like that happens?*

We loaded up two cars with only our most important items.

Before we left, my dad covered the furniture. It was strange, like a scene from a movie where people walk into a house that hasn't been lived in for a while, and everything is covered in white sheets.

We drove two hours away—about 120 miles from Harrisburg to Scranton, Pennsylvania. I'm not even sure if that was far enough to be safe, but that's where we ended up. A few days later, when the news said it was okay to return, we went home.

All three of the nuclear reactors have since been decommissioned. But whenever I fly into Harrisburg, I still see them from the plane and remember that time back in 1979.

WHATEVER I WAS GOING TO BE, I WAS GOING TO BE IT SOMEWHERE ELSE

In high school, I skipped on Senior Skip Day—except I wasn't a senior yet. Once again, I found myself ducking down, hiding in my boyfriend's car, when I saw my dad in the car next to us. *Jeez, another close call!*

When I look back, my behavior was all very innocent. Just look at what the kids are doing in this day and age—bringing guns and drugs into schools, shooting and killing people. The world has become a crazy place. I have to blame some of it on social media.

I'm so happy to have not grown up in this time of computers and iPhones. When we were kids, we dreamed of a telephone that would allow you to see someone when you talked to them. Ha! Now I see FaceTime come up on my phone and I hit the button—*declined!*

Pennsylvania was a great place to grow up, but I always knew I wanted to get out. It wasn't enough for me. I knew in order to accomplish more in my life, I had to go to a much bigger city.

Now I wasn't really one of those kids who knew exactly what I wanted to be when I grew up. I just knew *whatever I was going to be, I was going to be it somewhere else.*

Around age fourteen, I became interested in fashion magazines. I would comb through *Vogue* checking out the new styles and admiring the models' hair and makeup. One day I decided, *that's it—I'm going to be a model.* I had a long way to go before I could even think about accomplishing that goal and leaving Pennsylvania, but hey, a girl can dream!

All I knew was once I was out of high school, that was it for me. I hated school, so I already knew I wouldn't be going to college. Ohhh, if only I could tell my fourteen-year-old self anything, it would be *GO TO SCHOOL!*

But I was a free spirit at heart, and I don't think you can tame that. I figured all I had to do was find something I liked doing and could make money at. Easy, right?

EILEEN FORD

When I was eighteen, a friend was attending one of the local colleges. She told me about a bus trip to New York City to visit the museums. I asked if she thought I could get on that bus. She said, "Yeah, I think I'm allowed to bring someone." So I gathered up my portfolio and joined her. The bus arrived in front of the museum, and while everyone else was going inside, I waved goodbye to my friend and told her I'd meet her back at that spot before the bus left. And off I went to the Ford Modeling Agency.

I'd heard stories about Eileen Ford and how direct and to the point she could be with the girls who were coming in trying to be models. She told one of my friends, "Your nose is too big, and your lips are too small, and you'll never make it as a model." So I wasn't sure what to expect. I got called into Eileen Ford's office and sat in front of her as she combed through my very amateur portfolio. She looked at the photos, looked at me, and then looked back at the photos again. Then she shut the book and simply said, "Your look is too commercial for us. However, there are other agencies you could go see that you could probably work with." I was actually very happy with what she told me—it could have been way worse.

To this day I still remember going on that interview in a purple suit. Don't ask me how or why I wore that, but I remember it, and I'm sure I wore way too much makeup, too. Live and learn.

HEY, YA WORKIN'?

The first time I flew was in 1981. *My first plane ride!* They still allowed people to smoke, and there were those tiny ashtrays in the armrests...*again, fucking ashtrays!* I was headed to Las Vegas for the finals of the Miss English Leather Calendar Girl Contest, having won a local Miss English Leather Contest at a speedway in Pennsylvania. I remember being a trophy girl and handing out the trophies to the winners.

The Miss English Leather finals had just one winner, who told me I should have a nose job. *Bitch.* She ended up becoming Miss Louisiana. Then there were twelve other girls, one for each calendar month. I was one of them; I think Miss October because I remember pumpkins, and I hated the pic. But whatever—it got me on a plane, and it got me to Vegas.

Back then in Vegas, girls hung out all over the streets. There was a line of women sitting in front of my hotel on a cement wall. They were dressed in miniskirts and high heels, and a few had those 1980s short rabbit fur jackets. As I walked by, one of the ladies called out, "Hey, ya workin'?" I just looked at her and shook my head a little bit puzzled. Then I realized exactly what she meant, and I said, "No, I'm not working," to which she replied, "Well, you oughta be."

I took off running as fast as I could into the hotel lobby.

On the same trip, another contestant and I flagged down a taxi to go back to the hotel. We jumped in, and our driver turned around, took one look at us, and said, "Hey, girls! You ladies having a good night? You making money?"

I manage to find humor in just about everything in life. You have to, it's a survival tool for me. That was Vegas in the '80s, and you know what they say about Vegas...

ALWAYS THE BRIDESMAID...MISS PENNSYLVANIA

During that same time, I decided to enter the Miss Pennsylvania USA pageant. I think it was 1980 when I entered for the first time. I didn't even end up in the top ten. I was an amateur, and it was definitely my first rodeo, so I waited to re-enter again in 1982. That year, I was first runner-up to Miss Pennsylvania, and I also received a special award for Miss Photogenic. But that wasn't enough for me because I didn't get the crown.

So I proceeded to go back again in 1983 and 1984. Both of those years, I was once again first runner-up. After that my dad said, "Okay, I think you've had enough. I think it's fixed." *Of course* parents want to think that. Whatever the reason, I couldn't quite get that crown—that's just how it turned out.

It was like always being the bridesmaid but never the bride.

After the whole pageant experience I decided it was something I just wasn't cut out for.

So I moved on.

From there, I went on to do local modeling gigs, whatever paid. It didn't matter if I was modeling for a tool product or a fur coat company—whatever I could get, I did it.

I was in my very early twenties when I said to myself, *Okay, I have to go—this is it.* I needed something more in my life. And good thing I left because coming back a few years later, I ran into people I went to school with who were still there, still stuck in their same dead-end jobs, and very unhappy about it. I always say *you have to get out sooner than later, or you never will.*

But we all make our choices in life. I think you just have to have enough drive, gumption, or whatever you want to call it to get up, move, and make a better life for yourself—or at least try to.

There is never anything wrong with leaving and coming back. At least you can say you tried! But for me, once I was gone, I was gone. That was it—there was no turning back.

A close friend once asked me, "Why is it you always look at the big picture when I always look at the small picture?" I just kind of shrugged my shoulders and said, *"Why settle for less when you can have more?"*

Some people go for the gold. I like to go for the platinum in life.

Once I got to Los Angeles, there definitely was no turning back. In fact, after you've lived in LA, it's very hard to live anywhere else. The city is like a vacuum cleaner: it sucks you back in, no matter how hard you try to leave or how long you stay away. Something about it pulls you back in with a lot of force and holds a tight grip.

And that's exactly what it did to me. I stayed there for many years, in addition to living between Amsterdam and LA. At another point, I bought a house in South Florida and went back and forth between there and LA.

I ended up staying in my Florida home for about six months until I said to myself, *This place is for newlyweds and half-deads,* and I went back to Los Angeles for another twenty years!

But I'd been to South Florida before I ever went to LA...

THE SUGAR COOKIE

In 1984, I moved to South Florida with the sister of a friend from Pennsylvania. She wanted to move, and I did too, so off we went. Not long after arriving, probably two weeks, we were out clubbing and met two guys who invited us to come aboard a small boat called the Sugar Cookie and sail to the Bahamas. Here I was in my early twenties, living in Florida just a few weeks, and invited to go to the Bahamas! *Wow the Bahamas! Blue waters and lots of sunshine! Of course I'll go on your boat.*

I called my dad to tell him I was going to the Bahamas with some guys I just met. I gave him the name of the boat and told him I'd call him when I got there. Well, not long after we got on the boat, we ended up in a marina in Jacksonville because there were some mechanical issues. But I was having such a good time, I never called my dad to let him know I was going to be delayed.

My poor dad was worried to death, but I didn't know it. We didn't have cell phones back then, and dealing with a pay phone would have been way too much trouble.

The boat finally got up and running, and we were off to the Bahamas—about two weeks past our original date. It was a beautiful trip.

Growing up in Pennsylvania, I'd never seen clear blue water—only the Atlantic Ocean in places like Ocean City, Maryland, or Ocean City and Atlantic City, New Jersey. So when I first came to Florida and was offered a trip on a boat to the Bahamas, I was like *hell yeah.* To see the crystal clear blue waters that I had never seen before was amazing. We could see fish swimming below us—a sight you don't get in the murky Jersey coast waters.

It was so beautiful and peaceful, with the sun glimmering off the water, that I could have stayed there forever. And of course, *who needs a bathing suit when you are on a boat in the middle of nowhere?*

I could see all kinds of beautiful things I'd never seen before: fish swimming, coral, and for a while, we had dolphins following alongside the boat. We swam in the blue water, lay in the sun all day, and finally reached the Bahamas.

I think we ended up in the Exumas. We'd been on board the Sugar Cookie for three weeks, and, once on land, we were ready to get back to civilization. We wanted to go to Paradise Island and have some fun. The guys said the best way to get there would be to charter a small plane.

At that time, the Exumas were pretty primitive. We asked some locals how we could make a call. They pointed us in the direction of a little broken-down shack with a goat tied up outside. Turned out that was the phone company. We called to have someone get us off that island. Some really young-looking boy showed up in a tiny plane and flew us to Paradise Island. I can still sort of remember this tiny aircraft with what seemed like plastic windows that vibrated with the wind. The risks I took at that age!

When we reached Paradise Island, I finally called my dad. I'd put him through hell worrying about me—he hadn't heard from me for weeks. Also, the mother of the girl I was with was in contact with my dad. At some point, I think my dad had done enough worrying and decided he would call the Coast Guard because he knew the name of the boat.

But while the Coast Guard was en route to the boat, we were on the tiny plane en route to Paradise Island.

The Coast Guard found the Sugar Cookie in the Exumas with the two guys on board. They inspected the boat, and it turns out there weren't enough life jackets!

Later in life, I wondered what else those guys were carrying on board. I'm pretty sure they could have been running drugs. Maybe they dumped the goods before the Coast Guard arrived, or perhaps their cargo was well hidden. All they had told us was that they had to deliver the boat.

And what about the fact that they stayed up on watch every night looking for sea pirates? *Sea pirates?!* I'd never even heard of such a thing. Later, I learned the term referred to guys who rob boats looking for money and drugs.

But back then, I was in my very early twenties and wasn't thinking about much else except going to the Islands, drinking Rum Runners and Bahama Mamas, and having a great time.

I do believe I've caused quite a lot of overtime for my guardian angels throughout my life. And yes—I have angels around me. I'm not exactly sure who they are, but they are there, and I'm grateful.

JESSHEIM

While in the Bahamas, I was a little preoccupied with a lovely, long-haired, blond Norwegian guy named Arne (pronounced "ar na") I met while in Nassau. He worked on one of the Norwegian cruise ships that happened to be docked in the harbor. His father was one of the ship's captains. He was tall, thin, and very tan—and was hip, cool, and different for that time. I had loads of fun with him and his friends, who always managed to find the nude beaches while in the Islands.

As it would turn out, I was invited to spend a month with him and his family in the small town where they lived just outside Oslo, Norway. This was my first overseas trip! Jessheim was a lovely little village with doll-like houses. It was there that I learned to eat *Gjetost*, a brown Norwegian goat cheese with jam—it absolutely melted in your mouth. *Yum!*

Arne and I went out with all his friends in the evening, piling into a Mini and taking one designated driver who would not be drinking that night. The driving laws were very strict, so nobody wanted to take a chance on losing their license.

And Arne's mother was very sweet. She hand-crocheted a beautiful Norwegian sweater for me, which I still have in perfect condition some thirty-six years later.

The famous Vigeland Sculpture Park, Oslo, Norway.

It's been years since I talked to Arne. However, I did manage to track down one of his sons in Norway—on Instagram (of course)! I let him know I would be including his father in my book. It was sort of like pulling teeth, getting this kid to believe that I was a friend of his father's from long ago. First he asked me to send a selfie of myself right now. So I sent the photo. Then he said, "That's not you." I told him it was, in fact, me, and if he went to my website, he'd be able to see who I am.

In the meantime, I went to my garage, tore through the cabinets, and dug out the old photo albums I had with pictures of his dad and me, along with his grandparents and aunts. He said, "Wow, I never saw those photos," but he obviously recognized his father and the family.

The kid actually thought I was some sort of catfisher! I guess after he took a look through my website and realized I had a TV show at one point, combined with all the family photos I was able to come up with, he decided to believe me and said he would pass on the message. But, as a backup, I found Arne's sister on Facebook. I sent her a message as well. I haven't heard back from Arne as of yet, but when the book is finished, I'll send one to Norway, or *maybe I'll just deliver it myself.* After all, Norway is a beautiful country with gorgeous people, and I'm looking forward to returning one day.

FAIRY TALES AND FOREIGNERS

I have always had a thing for men with accents—especially foreigners! I'm not sure why, but I think it must have something to do with all the fairy tales I read as a kid. Most of the tales started out by saying, "In a land far, far away. there was a handsome prince..." Maybe that was the intriguing part of wanting to meet men in other countries—who knows? Whatever the reason, it's something I was highly attracted to and curious about, and another reason I enjoyed traveling to other countries so much.

I've met Swedish men who kind of sing when they speak, Norwegians who are very proud to be Vikings, Dutchmen who just love their *biertjes* (beer) and their women, French men with gorgeous accents that made me melt, and Italians who actually grabbed me on the streets. Giorgio from the shoe shop in Rome left two dozen roses at my hotel. A Greek man who really put on the extra charm and followed me to my hotel room with a rose as if he was on *The Bachelor*. (I told my aunt who I was visiting in Athens that I'd come to meet a Greek god, to which she said, "Michele, there are no Greek gods in Greece, only goddamn Greeks"!) I've met Persian men who are always impeccably dressed and doused in tons of cologne that lingers in the elevator long after they have stepped out, and Latin men who are very direct in telling you exactly what they want even if they only met you five minutes ago!

Maybe I was thinking I would find a frog just like in the fairy tales, kiss him, and have my handsome prince, but I think I found more frogs than princes in my travels.

It reminds of a joke: There was a woman hiking in the woods when she heard a voice say, "Pick me up, pick me up—down here, pick me up! Kiss me, and I'll turn into your handsome prince!" She looks on the ground and sees a talking frog. She picks him up and puts him in her backpack. The frog says, "No, no! What are you doing? You have to kiss me, and I'll turn into your prince!" The lady looks at the frog and says, "No thank you. At my age, I'd RATHER have a talking frog!"

Yes, I would too!

SOUTH FLORIDA, ONE BIG SPRING BREAK

South Florida was a big spring break place in the '80s, and I wanted to be a part of it. I remember the strip in Fort Lauderdale—the street at a standstill with traffic and spring breakers jumping on the hood of cars just for fun. Oh my gosh, what was I thinking getting caught in all of that?!

And then there were the bikini contests. You could actually make a living doing the contests on the weekends as long as you could make it from one to the next in time to enter. *Yep, like barhopping, but it was more like bikini-contest hopping.* The Candy Store, Penrods, Bootleggers...we would run from place to place!

Hey, $500 bucks to take a walk around a swimming pool? Not a bad gig! Again, *what was I thinking*—but I was young and enjoying life as I always have. And even a second or third place would still get a $100 or $200 prize.

Then at some point, I got bored with Florida and decided to try Los Angeles...*LA, here I come!*

PART II

Life Is All about Experiencing as Much as We Can

So You Know…

I DECIDED TO ENJOY LIFE THE MINUTE I LEFT HOME, AND once I started experiencing all that life has to offer, I realized there was no turning back. You can't go back to a small town once you experience so much more. I choose to look ahead out the windshield, not behind in the rearview mirror, and to keep moving forward!

During those years, I became very independent. I knew I'd always be able to survive on my own. Traveling to other countries taught me that wherever I am in the world, I can go with the flow—something I would never have learned from a textbook! I gained great respect for other cultures, from the translator I worked with for a month in Indonesia, who lived in a home with dirt floors, to the guy in Bali who I trusted in my early twenties to take me around on his own—driving me high into the mountains and through the rice paddies, stopping from time to time to pray at the altar he had set up on the dashboard of his van. Each place is unique and not to be forgotten.

Once I started really living, I wanted more! I always have and still do. It's as if nothing is ever enough. And I have been told that many times—mainly from men who say, "It's never enough for you." Well, *why settle when you can have more?* I needed to see the world and what it had to offer me because life is all about experiencing as much as we can.

PLAYBOY MODELS

In 1986, I moved to Los Angeles after doing a few stints as an extra on *Miami Vice* in Miami. I figured I would try my luck at modeling and acting in LA. My boyfriend had moved there and was spending his days pretty much getting beaten up and tossed around in an attempt to become a stuntman. So off I went to LA to join him.

I walked into the Playboy building on Sunset Boulevard my first week in town, went up to the reception desk, and said, "Hi, I wanna be a model." They sent me to the tenth floor to see a lady named Irena Kamal. She was a very lovely German woman, and we became close friends almost immediately. She was my booker during my years at Playboy, until she passed away in the early '90s. Irena sent me out on many auditions and castings. Sometimes a client would call and ask for only one girl, and she would immediately call me. She taught me the importance of always being on time and told me, "Don't be like the other girls! Do not stay out partying all night long, or you will not get booked!" I listened. Because of her, to this day I never show up late for an interview or an appointment—I'm always early. After all, they say being on time is late.

Photo shoot, Hollywood, California. Photo: Andy Pearlman Photography.

I wasn't quite sure what to think of LA. There were pretty people everywhere. The first time I walked into the ladies' room in one of the nightclubs, I stopped dead in my tracks at the sight of a line of beautiful women standing in front of the mirror, primping, and fixing their hair and makeup. I listened from the bathroom stall as they talked about a modeling job they'd just booked or the casting they went on earlier in the day. And then there was the talk of hair extensions and plastic surgeons. I left thinking I had to go in search of a plastic surgeon.

Early on, I went on the casting for the music video "California Girls." I was brand-new in LA, carrying around my portfolio with just a handful of pics. I walked into a room filled once again with beautiful women—they were everywhere.

We had to wear a bikini with high heels. I was nervous as hell when I walked into the room to meet David Lee Roth and had to dance around in front of him—*omg!!* I didn't book that gig, but every audition was an experience. You win some; you lose some. You just pick yourself up and go on to the next one because eventually, the gig will be yours. Keep moving forward!

AA

Another early-on audition was at a casting agent on La Cienega Boulevard. I walked into the room, signed in, and watched and listened as other girls walked in, happy to see each other. There were about five busy chatting about this and that, and how they all knew each other from some club or group that they were all connected to. So when I went home I said to my boyfriend, "I think I need to join this group that all these girls are in, maybe I would make friends."

He said, "What's the name of the group?" I said it was AA. He kind of smirked and said, "Oh, you do not want to be a member of that group. That's Alcoholics Anonymous!" I was like, "What's that?" I grew up in a small town in Pennsylvania and had never heard of AA. I didn't know anyone back then who was in it, so

I had no clue what it was. Young and naïve? Yes! You can learn a lot living in LA.

I thought driving and finding my way to the castings would be confusing. We did not have GPS back then, so we used the *Thomas Guide*. It was a big, thick book with maps and street names, and it was, in itself, confusing. The city was easy to maneuver, but then I had to deal with all of the freeways. The 405, which is also known as the San Diego Freeway, the 5 known as the Golden State, the 170 known as the Hollywood Freeway, the 101 also called the Ventura Freeway, the 10 known as the Santa Monica Freeway...and the freakin' list goes on. But somehow I managed.

Playboy Models sent me on jobs across the country as well as in Indonesia and Argentina, but most of my work was in Los Angeles. In the early days, I did everything from conventions, posters, calendars, print work, and commercial work to extra work, movies, and TV. I went to castings on a daily basis, and back then, I worked four or five days a week doing different gigs. I would run to one gig with a swimsuit under my clothes, then off to the next one with an evening gown in my bag, or maybe a business suit. Whatever the look, I was prepared.

THE FARMERS MARKET, MY SMALL TOWN IN THE CITY OF ANGELS

When I didn't feel like running back home to change for an audition, or if I had time to kill in between, I would stop at the good old Farmers Market on Third and Fairfax and do a quick change or grab a bite. It was a central point in the middle of LA and West Hollywood—close to most of the auditions, and one of the first places I discovered when I moved to Los Angeles. Thanks, Jeff Zeliger!

Now, this isn't your average farmers market with pop-up tents and vegetables and fruits only. This is a mom-and-pop kind of a place, with some of the businesses handed down from generation to generation. It originally started in 1934 but became something much more over the years.

You can find all kinds of great items at the Farmers Market: Thai, Cajun, Brazilian, French, and Italian food—and more. New York deli, ice cream, pizza, fresh baked goods, candies, nuts, fresh fruits and vegetables, as well as other goods like souvenirs, T-shirts, candles, and jewelry. There's even a guy who will repair your shoes.

In 2002, the Grove was built as an addition to the Farmers Market, with a walk of new shops, boutiques, department stores, and restaurants. But I still prefer the old, original 1934 area, where I can sit and have ready-made food from a number of restaurants, or a coffee early in the morning, and a glass of rosé later in the day. I was there on a daily basis and knew everyone by name, and they knew me.

One of the best things about the Farmers Market is it's a great place to people-watch. There are big busloads of tourists, old-timers who've been coming for years for their morning coffee meetings, celebrities, hipsters, and non-hipsters. And because CBS is just across the parking lot, you'll see executives and TV stars, as well as *The Price Is Right* audience waiting to get into the show.

It's still my most favorite place in LA. For me, it's like going to a small town within the city, and it reminds me of a Pennsylvania Dutch market we had where I grew up, called West Shore Farmers Market. I used to go there with my dad when I was very young. We'd get home-baked breads, fresh cheese, candies, and of course, pizza!

To me, the Farmers Market in Los Angeles seemed very similar. It was full of fruit and vegetable stands with different types of foods—the same as my childhood market. The only thing missing were the Amish!

It was also a very casual, laid-back kind of place, so different from the rest of Los Angeles that it almost seemed as if it didn't belong. It felt comfortable and safe, a place where I could get to know the owners on a personal level. In a city filled with glitz, glamor, and paparazzi, it had a hometown feel I loved.

Although it has changed some over the years, when I fly to LA, my ritual is still to visit the Farmers Market as soon as I get off the plane. I can't drive to my hotel without stopping at "Farmers," as I call it. I often arrive at noon and find myself wandering around shopping, having coffee, people-watching, or talking to my friend Scott who owns Bennett's Ice Cream. Later on, a friend will join me at the lovely French place called Monsieur Marcel for a glass of wine before finally heading off to my hotel hours later.

I have always said *if they built apartments right in the middle of the parking lot, I would be the first in line!*

If you're ever in LA and you can't find me, well, chances are you missed the Farmers Market, hence their slogan: meet me at Third and Fairfax! See you there!

BOOM BOOM

I was able to become a member of the Screen Actors Guild in 1987 when I did *Star Search* with Ed McMahon. I was one of the spokesmodels, and although I didn't win in that category, it was definitely a great experience—even if a bit nerve-racking being in front of a live television audience for the first time.

One of my first jobs was working with Tim Conway on a series of short videos, the first being *Dorf on Golf.* I played the dumb blonde role of "Boom Boom." Tim was the kind of guy who was just as funny in person as he was on TV. From the moment he opened the door of his trailer dressing room to meet me, he was hysterically funny and a little bit goofy.

I did a total of four different videos with Tim during the late '80s, and it was a great privilege to work with him. I ran into him years later at The Palm Restaurant in Los Angeles, when I was walking in and he was walking out. I said, *"Hey, Tim, it's Boom Boom,"* and I proceeded to introduce him to my boyfriend. Tim took one look at my boyfriend and said, "Hello, Mr. Boom Boom, how are you?"

IGUAZU FALLS, ARGENTINA

On set in Argentina at the Puerto Iguazu Falls.

In 1988, I was sent to the Iguazu Falls, which straddle Argentina and Brazil. Flying over is beyond spectacular. I was working on a film called *Los Kulies* and was in Argentina for more than a month. It was one of those low-budget B-movies where a girl runs through the jungle half naked, but *no, I wasn't toting a gun, and I wasn't topless.*

Iguazu is really and truly a sight to behold. It's part of a national park, and there are over 300 waterfalls that stretch approximately 820 miles and have a drainage basin of 24,000 miles.

Every day, I trekked from the hotel through the national park, then straight down a slew of cement steps. From there, I had to wade across the river until I reached a small island, where we spent the month shooting. The weather was very hot—110-plus degrees in the afternoon. The only shade came from a few lean-tos—like I said, *low budget.* But I didn't mind because I was working, getting paid, and exploring another culture at the same time. I also had young locals who didn't mind schlepping my backpack to and from the hotel every day for a small fee. They were happy to do it and excited to meet an American girl.

One of the most memorable things that happened to me on this trip was when the director said in his very heavy, lovely Latin accent, "Okay, Meechel, we will need you to swim in the Paraná River now for our next scene." *WTF?* I think I responded with something like, "Oh, sorry, but that wasn't in my contract!"

He said, "Don't worry about it. The piranhas are only above the falls, Meechel. They won't come down." I was thinking, *How the heck does he know if one, or two, or an entire school of piranhas might decide to drop over the falls? And guess what? I am NOT swimming in that river! That's a death I can avoid, thank you very much. Just fire me now, please!*

The director tried to persuade me a few more times but I flat out refused. All I could think about was piranhas nibbling on my toes. The male lead in the film did end up swimming in the river, and I can tell you he wasn't very happy about it at all.

But seriously, the Iguazu Falls are surrounded by beauty, wildlife, and natural hot springs that are simply amazing. My time there was a rare and memorable opportunity. If you happen to find yourself in Argentina, check out Puerto Iguazu Falls. But please don't swim in the Paraná River!

JAKARTA, INDONESIA

Visiting an orphanage while filming in Indonesia.

In 1988, Playboy Models asked if I would be interested in going on a casting for an Indonesian film. I thought, *Of course, who doesn't want to go to Indonesia?* I ended up booking the part and spending more than a month there.

Upon arriving at the airport in Jakarta, I was told to look for a man holding a sign with my name on it. Keep in mind, this was one of the first times I'd traveled to a strange land on my own, and here I found myself in an airport at the mercy of someone I didn't know. I still remember his name: Karsurianto Kwee—a.k.a "Kar"—and I'm sure I just spelled that incorrectly.

He was a very nice young man in his late twenties or early thirties who was to be my guide, driver, and host for the next thirty days.

Having just completed a long plane ride, I asked if he could point me in the direction of the restrooms. He pointed across the street to a building, so I walked across the street, opened the door, and went inside, expecting to find a toilet. Much to my surprise, there was nothing but a hole in the ground with two cement tiles on either side of the hole to rest your feet on while you squat—and no toilet paper, just a bucket of water. *Oh well!* As they say, when in Rome...

Some might find it disgusting, gross, or appalling, but I have learned over my years of traveling to many different places, if you want to fit in and be comfortable wherever you find yourself, you just have to go with the flow. So I did.

Jakarta, Indonesia, was a city with many sights and smells—and tons of traffic. It seemed like there were horns beeping constantly. I remember stopping at a traffic light, looking to my right, and seeing the local "barbershop": a man in a chair with a mirror tied around an old tree and another man shaving his face. At another stopping point, I looked to my left and saw food being served on glass plates from a cart. The customer would eat the food and hand back the plate, which the owner dipped quickly in a dirty bucket, before reusing it for the next customer. It all seemed very primitive to me, and at the same time interesting to watch.

Arriving at the hotel, Kar wanted my passport. I asked why, and he said, "We've had other actresses come and then just leave before the shoot was finished." I told him, "I can assure you I am not leaving, and I will not hand over my passport, but if you want me to hand over my passport, then I will be leaving."

I found it hard to sleep in Jakarta. A loudspeaker broadcast prayer and music to the whole area. The nights seemed long, and it was as if the prayer went on for hours. I saw lizards running around my room, squeezing under the cabinets and furniture, and strange bugs crawled around me as well.

I actually asked to be moved to a different hotel—one that wasn't so central to downtown! After all, I was spending many weeks there, and I wanted to be comfortable.

Sometimes I would walk into a public restroom and find women on the carpets, praying. It's always the experience of each culture's habits or customs that I love the most when traveling. Every culture is unique in its own way.

The film I worked on was a low-budget Indonesian comedy in which my voice was dubbed over in Indonesian. I have blessedly forgotten most of the details—it was so long ago! However, my niece's husband, Ben, just loves to dig up all my old movies, TV shows, and so on. Don't ask me how he finds this stuff. I have no clue. He recently found this exact old film and sent me a clip of a scene where I did some dreadful dance! *Oh, the memories...*

I took the job because I'd always wanted to see Bali, so once we wrapped, I headed there for a few days.

BALI

Bali was gorgeous—so lush and green. I watched a Balinese dance show one night, and the next day, I hired a local to take me on a tour. Bali offered stunning views everywhere! I saw women working in the rice paddies, some with children next to them. My guide showed me the beach, and then he took me to the local shops. After seeing some of the souvenirs, I asked him to take me to where they were made—high in the mountains. I told him I didn't want to go to where the tourists shopped; I wanted to actually see these things being made for myself. Off we went! I spent the day with him, which cost about twenty dollars back then.

At the end of the day, we arrived at a temple, which he said was a very sacred place. He said if a woman was menstruating, she would not be allowed to go inside the temple. As we were walking through the temple I heard noise and shouting, and then I heard money and change being thrown around. Next thing you know, we came upon a circle of men who were organizing a cockfight. I saw these poor birds with some kind of sharp object tied to their feet. It was completely shocking for me as an animal lover. I told my guide, "I have to leave." I thought this sacred place seemed less sacred than strange. But every culture is different, and what we might think is cruel and shocking is normal to others.

SPAIN

Playboy Models sent me to Spain in 1989 for a *Playboy Magazine* layout called "Travel Through Spain," which appeared in the December issue. I visited numerous cities, including Madrid, Barcelona, Jerez de la Frontera, Granada, and Ibiza over a period of two weeks.

I traveled from city to city in a small motorhome with my Spanish driver. He drove like he was Dale Earnhardt Jr. or Mario Andretti. This guy was fast—he steered the caravan like he was turning the corner in a Lamborghini or a Ferrari. I held onto anything I could grab for dear life! I know for sure I must've had guardian angels with me on that trip.

We took photos all day, and ate dinner late at night like typical Spaniards. Ibiza was the best. Dancing in bubbles late at night while shooting—crazy fun! In the afternoons, we would shoot a little more and end the day eating paella on the beach.

Photo shoot in Spain, 1989.

I remember *Playboy* wanting to get some shots of the bullfights. I had no idea what to expect. I sat there in the audience with the makeup artist listening to the crowds cheering and waiting for the event to start. The bull came running into the ring with all of his power, and then *boom,* the matador stabbed him with a long spear-like object. I was absolutely dumbfounded. I couldn't believe what I was seeing. We were told this maneuver gives the matador an advantage so the bull doesn't kill him. Well, I guess so! Anyone would have an advantage if their opponent was already injured.

Needless to say, I didn't want to stay and watch. Both the makeup artist and I ran out of there, and believe me, we couldn't leave fast enough. I know bullfighting is a huge part of the culture, but, like the cockfighting in Bali, I just can't stomach cruelty to animals. This is one part of travel where I can't go with the flow. It's not for me, ever.

I still can't remember if I was in Madrid or Barcelona when we were shooting on the street and a man drove past, looked over at me with a big smile on his face, and waved. The next thing you know, he ended up crashing his car and getting stuck on the median strip. Lucky for him he was okay, just a bit embarrassed. *Ahhhhh, the good old days of Playboy shoots.*

THE DUTCHMAN

In 1989, I met a man who was to become the absolute love of my life at that time. I will simply refer to him as The Dutchman.

Playboy Models used to put out a black-and-white photo book with all of their models' zed cards (photos). The book was sent to clients who might be interested in booking models for an event or photo shoot. One of the photographers, a man I knew named Don, approached me and asked if I would be interested in shooting a poster in Amsterdam. *Amsterdam? Of course I wanted to go to Amsterdam!* Don also told me he had a friend there who wanted to meet me. Honestly, I wasn't thinking about his friend—I was thinking, *I get to go to Amsterdam!* As it turned out, his friend was The Dutchman.

With my Dutchman, St. Tropez. Photo: Don Camp Photography.

The Dutchman had seen my zed cards in the Playboy Model photo book. He told Don, "When I like a girl, I like a girl like this one." So I went to the Netherlands thinking I was going to do a shoot for a poster, but the whole thing was a setup for me to meet the Dutchman...and it was a great setup!

At the time, I wasn't thinking about who I would be meeting, just that I wanted to explore another country. Little did I know that meeting this Dutchman would change my life. He was tall, handsome, very charming, a bit cocky at times, and a bit full of himself at other times. He was also kind and sweet and had one of the loveliest accents I have ever heard. I fell head over heels for him.

The Dutchman had security guards, drivers, private chauffeured bulletproof cars, and a private plane. To be honest, none of this impressed me as much as *he* impressed me. He was smart and hysterically funny, almost like a cartoon character. I have never laughed so hard in my life as when I was with him, and it was what I call a *real laugh*—the kind you never forget. He could walk in the door tomorrow, and I know he would still make me laugh, even after all these years.

I stayed In the Netherlands for two weeks the first time I met him. After that, I continued to go back and forth between Amsterdam and Los Angeles for the next four years.

The Dutchman lived life on the crazy side, especially for a businessman who was always in the newspapers. He spent many nights in smoke-filled pubs, drinking, laughing, and talking with his business associates. And then there were the women. Oh, the women who followed him around like a pack of wolves looking for their next victim! And of course he loved it. The first thing these women would ask me was, "Michela, when are you going back to the States?" I'd say, "Well, I only just arrived." Ha! *Take that!*

My afternoons were filled with shopping, lunching, and more shopping. I really learned to live life with The Dutchman and live it well. I had a love affair not only with him but also with Europe and all its culture and beauty.

When I think about him, I realize he taught me more than anyone else ever had. At times, I felt like Julia Roberts in *Pretty Woman*, at least the part where she upgraded her wardrobe on Rodeo Drive with the snobby sales associates and had a quick lesson in which silverware to use when at an important dinner.

That time in my life was truly the best. And even after all these years, I still keep in close contact with The Dutchman. There has always been a sort of unconditional love that I have for him, and at one point, he called our relationship "the impossible love." Impossible because after four years of spending nights in pubs and days shopping, I got bored. *Yes, bored.* I always do. I wanted to go back to the US. I wanted to finish what I started with my acting and modeling. I had given up so much by not being in LA and wondered, *What else am I missing?* Even though I loved shopping and the nightlife in Amsterdam, I wasn't ready to slow down and do just that—there was so much more to experience. So off I went, but we never forgot each other and always remain close, as he is only a phone call away.

THE RED LIGHT DISTRICT

Amsterdam is fun, crazy, wild, and wonderful. Of course, having lived there for four years, I'm partial, but there really are so many great places to see. Plus, the Dutch in general are full of life, humorous, free, open, and basically just very kind people.

My first stop upon arriving in Amsterdam had to be the red light district. Why, you ask? Because for years, it was all I'd ever heard about. Sitting in a private car, I was given my first look at that area of Amsterdam and all the sexy, scantily clad women in the windows. I quickly learned what it meant if the blinds in those windows were pulled down—the girls were busy, or, shall I say, *getting busy.*

Besides the windows, you can attend a live sex show pretty much any day of the week. (Yes, of course I did—I'm curious.) It's just like going to the movie theater.

It seems like I'm a magnet for the odd, curious, and eccentric—they find me wherever I go. Once, while walking down the street in Amsterdam, I was approached by an odd character with an English accent who fell to his knees in front of me, put his hands together like he was praying, and said, "Please, can I be your sex slave?" I ran away from him as fast as I could, but the funny thing is that almost two years later, on a different street in Amsterdam, I ran into him again. Once again, he fell to his knees and made the same request. *Not sure what that guy was smoking*—after all, it was Amsterdam, and "coffee houses" are what the city is famous for.

THE "COFFEE HOUSES"

Good times in Amsterdam. Photo: Don Camp Photography.

The coffee houses attract millions of visitors from all over the world each year. The most famous one is The Bulldog. I'm not sure why they even call them coffee houses, because I've never really seen anyone drink coffee in one. They are primarily for buying and smoking weed. The minute you walk in, the aroma of marijuana is so strong that you can almost get stoned just standing in the doorway.

Choose your smoke from the menu, and off you go—literally! I once got a T-shirt that said, "Why drink and drive when you can smoke and fly in Amsterdam?"

Now, in the late '80s and '90s, I remember seeing these stickers in the taxi cabs that read, "Yab Yum!" Being the inquisitive person that I am, I asked The Dutchman to take me there one night. He was happy to do it. It was basically a nightclub where men could purchase champagne for the working girls and possibly purchase a little more than that if they desired.

But what I remember most of all is a burly motorcycle man from the Amsterdam chapter of the Hells Angels. He walked up to me and squeezed me in a tight hold. I said, "Sir, let go," and he squeezed harder. Well, as my ribs were cracking and I was writhing in pain, I poured the glass of champagne I was holding over his head and then popped him a good one right in the face! He released his grip on me right away.

Because he was who he was, The Dutchman got worried, and the security quickly escorted us out of there, not knowing what might happen next. As luck would have it, a few weeks later, I ran into that same Hells Angel. He tapped me on the shoulder, and I turned and thought, *Oh shit.* But he said in a very kind voice, "I'm sorry, and I apologize." We shook hands, and I think I may have said something like, "Let's keep the peace."

But that wasn't the first run-in I'd had with that motorcycle club.

On another night when my friends had gone ahead to the casino, there was a Hells Angel couple who offered to give me a ride. I accepted. Once we were driving, they started laughing and said, "You're coming with us!" I wondered, *Am I really being kidnapped by Hells Angel members?* Yep, I was. I ended up in some private clubhouse bar, where I had to ask the bartender the address and if I could use the house phone. (We didn't carry cell phones that much in '89, and they wouldn't have worked in Europe anyway.)

The funny thing is years later, I would host a motorcycle show called *American Thunder* and became friends with some of the club members. When I told them I had punched a very famous member in Amsterdam they were like, "Nooo way!" I told them not to worry—we made up!

CANNES

Ooh là là, the French Riviera!

Très chic! Nothing better than lying on the beach, drinking champagne, with full service at your feet.

Cannes in the late '80s and early '90s was an amazing place. Now, don't get me wrong: it still is a beautiful place, but in the last ten years, it has changed and become much more commercial than it was back then.

Still, I love it, if for nothing else than for the greatest memories of all—again, traveling with The Dutchman! Our holidays or weekends to Cannes gave us a much needed break from the overcast, cold, rainy days in Amsterdam.

And new places to enjoy my shopping!

I think shopping was pretty much my hobby back then. In fact, The Dutchman used to refer to me as "the shopping monster." A friend of mine once went with me to Paris and said,

"Your eyes become crazy, and you focus in on something when you walk into a boutique or the Galeries Lafayette in Paris. Then you pounce like a tiger!"

There was a time when I came back from France with so many extra bags that they wouldn't fit in the luggage compartment on The Dutchman's private plane. We had to cram them into the bathroom, which meant that no one could use it for the two-and-a-half-hour flight from France back to Amsterdam. *What can I say?* There were so many beautiful things in Europe that I could not find in the States. I have since cut back on my shopping habit, at least until I'm back in France again.

I loved stepping off the plane in France. The ambiance in the South was lovely. Drinking coffee on the Boulevard de la Croisette—just the names were enough for me.

I remember all the lovely aromas in France, walking past the perfumeries or looking in the bakery windows and taking in the smell of fresh baked chocolate croissants—*pain au chocolat*, as they call it. And in between, all these amazing smells would come from a cheese shop with some of the tastiest cheeses, along with loaves of French bread. *Heaven!*

I always enjoy sitting and people-watching, whether it's on the beach or at a small café, watching the old men play bocce ball in the park or the French women sashaying down the Rue d'Antibes.

Someone once told me that when a French woman walks into a room, everyone looks. It doesn't matter if she's a beauty or not; it can be something as simple as how she ties her scarf, twists her hair back, or how she saunters that catches people's eye.

I once had a friend from Lyon, France, who I knew in LA. She owned a very cute boutique on Melrose Avenue. She wasn't exceptionally beautiful, but let me tell you, when she walked down the street, people noticed. Her hips would swing from side to side, her shoulders would move in a way I can't duplicate, and she owned the street.

I kind of think everyone should walk into a room like they own it. *Why not? Life's too short not to get noticed!*

CANNES FILM FESTIVAL

Walking the red carpet at the Cannes Film Festival, 1990. Photo: Don Camp Photography.

From 1989 to 1991, I was lucky enough to experience the Festival du Film in a very spectacular way: aboard the *Fiffanella*, a 132-foot Feadship superyacht. It was not a shabby way to attend the festival, especially for the first time, and probably one of my most memorable experiences ever. I was wined and dined, and I walked the red carpet at the Palais, attended celebrity parties, lunched with the mayor of Cannes, and even ended up in a few French newspapers and magazines.

Having the opportunity to screen some of the films before they hit the theaters was something special. There were so many parties and events to attend. One evening at a party in the Carlton Hotel, a girl I knew from LA approached me and said, "Hi I'm staying in the harbor on my friend's yacht next to yours. He saw you and asked me to give you this gift." She then handed me a box. Inside was a beautiful diamond Cartier Panthère watch!

I said, "Oh my, tell him thank you, but you have to return it to him. I'm here with The Dutchman, and I'm sure he wouldn't appreciate it if I accepted a gift from another man." I still remember The Dutchman's words: "What an idiot that guy is!"

Years later, when I was no longer with The Dutchman, the man from the yacht happened to find me via a photographer we both knew. The man's name was Jurgen and he was from Germany. We ended up having dinner in Miami. He sent a limo to pick me up and again gave me a piece of jewelry, this time a sapphire and diamond ring. I said, "I just want to tell you that I never accepted that beautiful watch you sent to me." He looked confused, and I explained I'd returned it to the girl.

He smiled a bit and said, "I knew it! I knew she kept the watch!"

Imagine all these years later, he thought I had that watch. And people always say don't shoot the messenger—ha!

When we were not at the parties or screenings, we spent our days watching photographers chase down topless sunbathers. It's impossible to be topless during the film festival unless you want to get swarmed by the paparazzi, especially the American ones. I remember one afternoon walking down the Croisette when all of a sudden, a girl ripped off all her clothing—and yes, I mean *all*—climbed on the hood of a Mercedes, and posed in the nude. It was a traffic-stopping stunt.

I think it's a rumor, but the story goes that Brigitte Bardot was supposedly discovered while sunbathing topless on a beach in the South of France, and the rest was history—she became famous and put Saint-Tropez on the map. So there were women who would literally throw themselves to the paparazzi in the hope of getting noticed and becoming famous.

At times, we would actually see Brigitte Bardot at the open air market in Saint-Tropez, long after her glory days. It seemed like there were photos of the beautiful icon everywhere in the South of France.

After all these years, I still manage to make my way back to the South of France now and then. I still enjoy people-watching along the Croisette and shopping on the small quaint streets of Saint-Tropez. I miss the smell of the South, the salt air, the coffee and croissants in the morning, and boats on the Mediterranean, so I satisfy my appetite with a trip whenever I can. I still lie on the same beach and watch the waves roll in and out. I remember the amazing times I had so long ago and dream of the new ones I will make while I'm there.

WHERE'S THE TOP?

The first time I went shopping for a bathing suit in the South of France, I asked the sales associate, "Where are the tops?"

She said, "Oh, we only sell bottoms."

I found it funny, but once again, *when in Rome!*

Back in the late '80s and early '90s, most of the women on the beach were topless. I think that trend started in the '60s but has since stopped. Women no longer go topless on the French beaches, and I'm not sure what happened.

I thought it was great that you didn't even have to stick to a certain section—you could go anywhere on the beach without a top.

Early in the morning, there was a woman who must have

been in her eighties who came every day to swim in the sea. She was always topless when she swam, and I thought to myself, *Good for her.* She'd most likely swum that way her whole life, so she wasn't changing now just because she'd aged and her body had changed. That was the greatest thing about it—she was confident and didn't have any hang-ups.

The Americans on the beach would stare, point, and laugh like a bunch of unsophisticated tourists who couldn't believe what they were seeing. I wanted to say to them, "Men, put your eyes back in your head, and women, get over it! After all, you are in France!"

I said to myself, *If you can't beat them, join them! Why not? Life is meant to experience everything.*

One time, I was in Saint-Tropez and saw a gentleman who looked to be in his seventies walking down the beach completely naked! Yep, everything was swinging in the wind, and I'm not talking about his hair. How great it was to see people being so free.

In other parts of Europe like Holland, I would see moms and dads totally naked, digging in the sand with their kids. That was a little weird for me because I just couldn't imagine being at the Jersey shore with my dad building sand castles naked by the shore. Oh, the thought!

THE USS *DWIGHT D. EISENHOWER*

Spending time in Cannes during the film festival was always a unique and interesting experience back in the day. From the contortionist who would walk the Croisette performing for all who gathered to the topless girls posing on the beach for the paparazzi, I saw it all. Attention seekers everywhere during that week made people-watching even more entertaining.

The USS Dwight D. Eisenhower. Photo: Don Camp Photography.

My first year at the festival, we stayed in the harbor. Docked not too far away was an aircraft carrier—the USS *Dwight D. Eisenhower.*

On a daily basis, I'd see sailors tendered in from the *Eisenhower.* They'd walk past our boat sometimes and wave or say hello. I kept seeing the same guys, and we eventually struck up conversations.

It was nice seeing my fellow Americans in France and having an opportunity to chat with some of them. It seemed like they were everywhere walking through the streets of Cannes. It made us feel safe. I suppose it must have been a nice break from their daily routine to be docked so they could get off the ship and interact with civilians, if only for a short time.

Eventually, the captain invited me to tour the enormous ship. It was amazing and even bigger once on board. The crew escorted me around the ship and explained what daily life was like on board for months at a time.

The guys were respectful, hardworking men doing a great service to our country, and they were nothing but a pleasure to meet and talk to. I stayed on board a few hours touring and taking photos with them. Years later, I was still receiving letters from some of the sailors who then watched me on *American Thunder*.

Even with all the craziness and all the celebrities the film festival brings, being able to tour the *Eisenhower* was definitely the highlight of the film festival for me that year. It was such a great experience and one I will always remember.

THOUGHTS ON CANNES

About Cannes: if you're looking for a lot of action like surfing or jet skiing and nightclubs, forget it! Not to say that those things don't exist in the South, but Cannes is a very glitzy and glamorous place. Think high-end, upscale chic. At times it can be a bit boring, but fantastic boring! Yes, there is a beach, but I wouldn't exactly refer to Cannes as a beach town. The clientele are much more fabulous than your typical beachgoers, although that has changed somewhat in the last ten years or so.

The beach itself is nothing special. For me, it was always about the people and especially the amazing service you receive while enjoying your day lounging on a beach chair and having everything at your feet. Of course, you pay for this comfort, but it's all very worth it. Whatever you want—they will service your every need. You won't find champagne or wine being served in a paper cup, and your salad will be brought right to your beach chair on a china plate. No plastic on this beach!

People are high-end and stylish in every way, even if they are just enjoying a day in the sand. If you look around, you'll spot designer everything—from the clothes on their backs to the sunglasses on their heads, to the expensive jewelry and watches that glimmer and dance when the sunlight hits them.

Nannies play in the sand with the children while the parents enjoy fine dining during lunch. Even the dogs partake in steak tartare from china plates while eating at the table.

That's France, that's Cannes, that's fabulous at its best!

PART III

The Walls Come Down

So You Know...

STANDING IN FRONT OF THE BERLIN WALL WAS A BIG DEAL. Taking a small hammer and chipping away, watching the tiny pieces of wall fly, I felt almost as if I were helping people escape to the other side. Even though the borders had already been opened, the wall was still there. So I chipped away, imagining what people had endured for so many years being trapped on one side or the other. If I'd been in that situation, I think I would have had to tunnel my way out.

This was a time in my life when I became more aware of a connection I have with the "other side." By the young age of twelve, I'd already experienced important people dying and had realized life can be cut off from us at any moment. Back then, I was afraid of death. However, as I got older, I read books about death and dying, and I no longer feared it. Plus, I had always felt angels around me. I'd never really been superstitious, not in the way most people think, but that changed a bit when I lived in LA in a house filled with spirits.

I've kept some of my stories to myself for many reasons, but just like the Berlin Wall, it's time for the barrier to come down. I have never told my story about Brunei until now. Almost every girl I knew who had been to Brunei wanted to return—the money, the jewelry, the prince, the lazy days of sunning by the pool, getting paid to do absolutely nothing. I'm glad I went—both times—and I'm even more thrilled that I kept living my life with my eyes on the road ahead because that led me to some truly great experiences.

THE BERLIN WALL

Chipping away at the Berlin Wall, 1989.

It was November 1989 when I heard about the Berlin Wall coming down and the borders opening up between East and West Germany. I was living in Amsterdam at the time. My business manager from Los Angeles was visiting, so we thought we'd go to Berlin and get a piece of the wall.

The border had just opened, and people from the East were

crossing into the West, some for the first time ever! I can't imagine what that would have been like for the East Germans. We'd heard that all the fresh produce was always sold out at the markets. Their clothing styles were very dated, and we heard stories of how Germans had been parted from loved ones—each one stuck on a different side of the border when it closed in 1961.

We booked a flight from Amsterdam to Berlin and stayed the weekend to explore the city and see the wall. We took a cab to the wall and watched as people chipped away at the graffiti to take souvenirs. We decided to do the same. We walked up to an area of the wall on the west side and started chiseling away with a hammer we'd purchased at a local shop.

We must have been at it for about ten minutes when one of the guards from the watchtower started flashing lights at us. Our taxi driver, who was waiting, said we had to leave because we were not allowed to be in this area. I jumped into that taxi as fast as I could, and we sped off. I looked back, thinking we might be chased by the guards. I did manage to get a few pieces of the wall. To this day, I'm not sure where they ended up. I gave most of them away, but at least I got a photo of the experience.

Thanks for the memories, Berlin!

ROME: ROSES IN THE BIDET

In the late '80s, I traveled to Rome with a girlfriend from Holland. We had a fabulous time walking around the city, exploring the ruins of the Colosseum, the Vatican and, of course, shopping.

We found a little shoe shop along one of the small streets and went inside. I was like a kid in a candy store—all kinds of beautifully made Italian shoes! I couldn't pick just one pair. *One doesn't go with every outfit.* It was heaven for me, and it was also during my "shopping monster" days.

After I picked out about ten pairs of shoes and they were piled high on the counter, I realized my credit card was back at the hotel. So I asked the owner of this little shoe shop if he would please hold them for me until I returned. He said, "Of course I will. Please give me your name and the name of the hotel that you're staying at."

My girlfriend and I left and shopped around a little more before returning to the hotel to pick up the credit card. Upon arriving back at the hotel, I discovered two dozen red roses waiting for me. Who could they be from? I opened the card attached, and it read, "With love from Giorgio in the shoe shop." Boy, Italians work fast!

Because we were running out of time before the stores closed and I needed to get all my shoes, I took the roses, filled up the bidet like a vase, and plopped them in the water. That bidet never looked better!

In the evenings, we'd choose one of the cafés that we passed along the way to have dinner. One evening as we sat and ate, a table of Italian men was staring at us. At one point, I got up to use the restroom, and then I heard a knock on the stall door. I said, "Someone is in here," and then one of the gentlemen handed me roses underneath the stall door. It took some nerve to walk into a ladies' room, but I guess that's how they did it in Italy.

When we were finished and the waiter gave us the check, another Italian gentleman walked over, picked it up, and said, "I insist." *Maybe I should have stayed in Rome a little longer!*

THE CONCORDE

In 1990, I was in a hurry to leave Amsterdam for a photo shoot back in the States, on the East Coast. I'd heard about this plane called the Concorde that could get you from Europe to the US in just under 3.5 hours. So I flew from Amsterdam to France and had the privilege of jumping on board the Concorde. My flight from Amsterdam was delayed, but they held the plane for me. I walked on board after everyone had already been seated, and the other passengers were staring me down, as if to say, "How could you be late? Don't you know this is the Concorde?"

The Concorde was very skinny on the inside and had maybe one hundred seats. It was all one class and very expensive to fly. Of course, regulars wanted to be up front because of the privilege attached to first class front seats. I think I was somewhere in the middle. I just couldn't get over how limited the space was. And it was noisy, too. But hey, I was on the Concorde, getting to New York from Europe in record time!

I sat back, relaxed in my little seat with a glass of champagne, and waited for takeoff. There was some sort of digital device in the front of the plane that showed how fast we were actually going. The Concorde speed was 1,341 miles per hour. It was fabulous, and I'm pretty sure I walked off that flight with a big smile on my face!

SPIRITS AND SUPERSTITIONS

I have long been superstitious about many things, including about the number thirteen, which some people actually consider a lucky number. I do own a pair of motorcycle boots with skulls that say "Lucky 13," and for some reason, I don't feel those boots are bad luck.

The letter "M" in my name is also the thirteenth letter of the alphabet. But as far as anything else associated with the number, let's just say *I proceed with caution.*

For instance, take Friday the thirteenth; you'll never see me flying on that day if I can help it. I also won't sit in a seat in the thirteenth row on an airplane except as an absolute last resort, which would then require a double or even triple prayer.

Then there is the old superstition of walking under a ladder, and to this day, I will not do it. I prefer to go around, just in case.

When I see a black cat running in front of me as I'm driving down the street, I usually stop and turn around. I don't know what such a crossing is supposed to do, but I figure there must be something to it.

I'm also superstitious about getting on a motorcycle without saying my motorcycle prayer.

I don't think I was very superstitious growing up, and I didn't think much about ghosts, except for the costumes on Halloween. When I moved to LA, though, that began to change. I would hear stories of old Hollywood hotels like Château Marmont or The Roosevelt Hotel where celebrities had died, and for one reason or another, those celebrities could still be heard or seen.

I didn't think much of it—they just sounded like the typical paranoia stories.

That is, until the ghosts moved in with me!

LA CASTANA DRIVE

In 1990, I leased a house in the Hollywood Hills, right at the top of Nichols Canyon near Woodrow Wilson Drive, on a small street called La Castana. The place was a beautiful, newly built, two-story, white, Mediterranean-style home of approximately 4,000 square feet.

I wasn't there very often because I traveled between LA and Amsterdam, but I had a live-in housekeeper who stayed to watch my small dogs and parrots.

The first year, I noticed the alarms in the house went off

frequently, but I attributed those incidents to windy nights or came up with other reasons.

Besides the alarms, I would hear footsteps on my roof, which would have required someone to have a pretty tall ladder.

Once in the afternoon, when a girlfriend and I were on the second floor, we heard footsteps in the kitchen downstairs. I said, "Oh my gosh, someone's in the house." My parrots were going crazy, and the dogs were barking. As we made our way slowly down the stairs, proceeding with caution, I saw my dog looking up and barking at the air. *Um...why?*

I'd also hear noises that sounded like someone tossing small stones or marbles that rolled across my roof. And I wasn't the only one who heard these noises; my family and friends did, too.

When I first leased the house, before I hired my housekeeper, I decided I needed to hire a security guard. Yes, I really did that. I called one of those rent-a-security-guard places, just like they use in the malls. I told the company I needed a guy to come to my home every night when it got dark and to stay until the very early morning, right before dawn. (No, I'm not paranoid, lol.) Then it would be okay for him to go home.

They sent me one guy who sat in the same spot on my couch every single night watching TV for a week, until there was an indentation left on the couch cushion. So I asked for a new security guard. I was a bit high-maintenance in those days— actually, *very* high-maintenance.

The second guy arrived with a briefcase. But It wasn't your typical briefcase—it was kind of thick, more like a mini suitcase. I thought, *This guy has weapons in that box, and what if he uses them on me?!* So as I passed through my kitchen to make my way upstairs to the bedroom, I pulled a large knife out of the drawer, thinking, *Okay, great, now I might need to protect myself not only from the spirits but also from the security guard as well!*

It was about 3 a.m. when I got a buzz from the intercom. The security guard said, "Excuse me, ma'am, but I went out onto the balcony to take a smoke, and I locked myself out." *Omg, really? He woke me up from my beauty sleep?!* After he locked himself out, he had to climb over the balcony to the front gate to buzz me. Needless to say, that was the end of renting a security guard for the night!

Then there was the night that I looked out at the swimming pool, and many of the large terracotta pots on the deck were just rolling around on their own. I looked at the trees, and the leaves were all still. Go figure.

I think at that time Westec Security must have thought I was a nutcase—I called them so often.

My live-in housekeeper didn't speak a word of English, yet somehow we always managed to understand each other. The funny thing is, one night when the alarms went off, she ran up a huge flight of stairs, burst into my room holding a broomstick, and yelled, "Meeechel, what happened?" Something scared the English right out of her.

When she went back to Mexico for a month to visit her family, I hired a lady from the Philippines. She kept telling me about the footsteps she would hear in the kitchen when only she was home.

By this time, I was trying to forget all the activity happening in my house. After all, I was often in Europe for weeks at a time, only returning to my LA house for a week here or there.

At times, I thought I heard talking in my ear as I slept. Other times, I ended up going to a hotel just to get a good night's rest.

One day, a neighbor of mine and her stylist came over to visit, and they looked through some of my clothing. Later when I ran into her husband, he told me that when they walked up the staircase to the second floor, a chill came over them as if they were being watched and were not alone. That was the feeling I had most of the last year that I lived in the house.

I called my brother to come visit. I wanted to know if he experienced the same thing; plus, I was just scared out of my wits. He spent about a week with me and told me I was nuts. He didn't hear anything, he didn't see anything…or so he said. He waited until after my lease was up and I had moved out before telling me, "I didn't want to tell you while you were living in the house, but a few nights when I was sleeping, I felt like there was somebody at the bottom of the bed watching me. You were already freaked out enough, so I decided to wait to say anything."

Long ago when I first moved to Los Angeles, I was told some homes in the Hollywood Hills were built on Indian burial grounds. I don't know if it's true, but some sort of energy was there in my newly built, never-lived-in house.

I also heard a story about a tragedy that happened in the neighborhood. A family had lived just around the corner from my home. The father returned from work one day and killed his wife and two of their children. The third child hid under the bed, watching everything. That child survived.

He grew up and still owned the house. Supposedly, he came back and started to remodel the home. I am convinced that while the remodeling was being done, those spirits moved over to my house. Perhaps they were a little lost?

HEY, YA WORKIN'? BUDAPEST

It wasn't just Vegas where I was approached about being a working girl. On several occasions, I traveled with The Dutchman from Amsterdam to Budapest, where he was the honorary consul to Hungary for Amsterdam. Once, we checked into the hotel, went up to our room, changed, and went out for a dinner meeting.

We came back late at night, me in my short dress, he in his business suit and jumped on the elevator only to have a hand stop the elevator door from closing. It was a big security guy who said, "Excuse me, madam, you cannot go up to the room with this gentleman."

The Dutchman, being The Dutchman, said a few choice words, hit the button, and closed the door on the guy. We went up to the room, and a few minutes later, there was a very loud knock on the door, the kind you hear in movies when the police arrive.

The Dutchman opened the door and said, "Can I help you?"

The guy said, "Yes, this girl is not registered with us to this room," insinuating I was one of the local hookers. *Really?*

I said, "Do you think that I'm going to fly all the way from California to Hungary to be a prostitute? After all, I live much closer to Las Vegas, and I'm sure the money would be better."

It was all because when we checked into the hotel, I didn't show my passport—but then again, they never asked for it. The next morning, the hotel manager apologized profusely.

I actually find it quite amusing, especially looking back all these years later. Even my dad got in on the hooker thing. One evening, my older sister and I were going out. She has always been more conservative than I am, and at that time in her life, she wore a lot of suits. So here we come, me in a mini dress and her all buttoned up in a freakin' suit. My dad took one look at us and said, "Oh, there goes the nun and the hooker, out for the evening." You gotta love my dad!

I have always considered myself to be pretty thick-skinned. After all, I'm a mix of German, Scandinavian, and Lithuanian. If I had to pick which one of those makes me tough, I suppose it's a toss up between the German and the Viking.

I believe you need to have a sense of humor in life and just let things roll off your back, which not all women are able to do. But I try to find humor in most things.

THE COMMUTE: LA TO AMSTERDAM

It was a great experience to live in Amsterdam and learn about the Dutch culture. For instance, bicycles were their means of transportation, whether they were going to work, picking up kids from school, or going to the market. I realized back then how easy we had it as Americans, even just running simple errands.

Yet they always seemed so happy. I did the best I could to learn their language, or at least some of it. I would sit and listen intently, trying to figure out what was being said. Then when I would come back to the States, and I would tune everyone out in public until I realized I could actually understand what they were saying. It was a weird transition sometimes.

During those years when I went back and forth between Los Angeles and Amsterdam, European life just seemed easier and less stressful. When I went to Amsterdam, I would book out at my agency, letting them know I wasn't available for auditions and "go-sees." When I returned, I'd let the agency know I was back and would take jobs while I was in the States, if they offered enough money.

I missed a lot by being in Amsterdam so much. Out of sight, out of mind. I would run into producers at the film festival in Cannes, and they'd say, "Hey, we were looking for you." At the time, I had no clue who they were, and I really didn't care.

It was after almost four years of travel between Los Angeles and Amsterdam, spending my days lunching and shopping and most nights sitting in a smoky pub with a bunch of Dutch businessmen, that I decided I was simply bored.

Although I loved The Dutchman to death, I was aware of everything in my own life that I was giving up to spend time in Amsterdam. Being there was holding me back. I still had so much more to do and so many places to see. After all, I was only twenty-seven when I met him.

So I told him I had to go back to Los Angeles to work. I missed it, I missed my friends, the auditions, working, and, of course, the Farmers Market! Some people would think I was nuts (I am) to leave such a luxurious lifestyle of basically doing nothing. But doing nothing 24/7 just isn't my thing. My mind works all the time, and the wheels are always turning. I can't let boredom set in on me.

Within a few months of returning to LA, I auditioned for this gig in Brunei...

BRUNEI (YES, *THAT* BRUNEI)

Sometime in the early '90s, a close friend who was a photographer in Los Angeles, someone I had known and trusted for many years, approached me about a woman who was holding auditions for a trip to the home of a royal family. I said, "Tell me more."

Basically, they were bringing women to Brunei, to the home of Prince Jefri, the brother of Sultan Hassanal Bolkiah. The job entailed attending parties by night and having free time during the day.

It sounded too good to be true, but I'm a curious person, so I decided I would go to the audition to get more details.

I met with a woman who worked directly for Brunei's royal family, the House of Bolkiah, and took care of the properties they had in Beverly Hills.

She said the royals had been having these parties for years. The women who attended them had been mostly Asian women from different parts of Malaysia, but now the royals were interested in having American women.

She said any of the American women who came were considered to be VIPs, and we didn't have to worry about anyone approaching us for sexual favors. Apparently, the women who came from other countries were expected to be with any of the men who approached them. Some were sent to Brunei by their families, while others came on their own—mostly from poor backgrounds with the desire to make a better life for the entire family. Allegedly some of these women made so much money going to Brunei that when they returned to their own country, they were set for life.

After asking many questions, I ended up agreeing and was put on a waiting list. The list was long, and only a handful of women were selected to go at one time. A few months later, I received a call and was told to be ready in thirty days. We received a payment upfront so we could take care of some of our bills before we left and make all our arrangements for being out of town for four to six weeks. About five girls traveled with me, most of whom were models and actresses from LA.

We flew into Singapore and spent the night. Singapore is a very clean city, and I couldn't help but notice the ads in the magazines that said "$500 fine for gum chewing." No wonder the place was so clean!

The following day, we flew into Brunei, a small, independent, oil-rich country in southeast Asia. We were escorted to a huge palace, part of an enormous property with many homes on the grounds. Once inside the palace walls, we were taken to one of the homes where we would stay for the coming weeks. The homes had four bedrooms each and were at least 3,000 square feet. The main palace itself was massive and overly decorated with solid gold statues and gold spun into the carpeting.

Each home had a house lady or two who would provide us with whatever we needed. They gave us fresh fruit daily, along with pans of freshly cooked Malaysian foods. We could ask for essentially whatever we liked, and it would be delivered to us. There must have been at least six homes on the property, all occupied by girls from different countries. During the day, we could use the gym or lie by the pool, but we had to stay within the walls of the palace so as not to draw attention. Once, a few of us received special permission to go into the city with one of the palace drivers. We had to be covered up from head to toe and only had a short time to shop around. As Americans, we probably would have stood out.

Gurkhas wearing camouflage uniforms patrolled the property. They seemed to be hiding and blended in with the trees. They were there to protect the royal family, and you never knew when one would pop out of the bushes.

Bringing girls to the palace was always "the big secret"! Prince Jefri, who also liked to be called Robin, was known as a sex-obsessed playboy. His yacht was named *Tits*, and two smaller boats used to ferry guests were named *Nipple 1* and *Nipple 2*. He was more than extravagant and more than eccentric with his spending. He was also the finance minister for his brother the sultan.

Whenever the sultan came to the palace, we were sent into hiding and could not leave the houses. There would be no gym or pool time, and the curtains were closed. We were not to be seen.

The thing is, we never knew when the sultan might arrive, so we'd sometimes hide out all day. When we heard the sound of the helicopter, we knew he was on the property. Supposedly, he had no idea that Prince Jefri had so many women around, but I found that hard to believe. There were stories of the prince offering women to the sultan, but again, they were only stories...

After the sultan left the palace, everything would resume as normal. We could come out of the houses once again.

Every night at 10 p.m., we had to attend a party, which consisted of approximately thirty Asian and six American women. We each sat in a different area of the room, but we Americans did talk with some of the other girls.

There was food, music, dancing, and karaoke. If you got called for karaoke, you *had* to sing. I was so happy no one ever called me up for that one!

There was also alcohol, which I found funny, because alcohol is supposed to be illegal in Brunei. But nothing seemed illegal at the palace. The parties usually ended sometime around 2 a.m., when we would be allowed to go back to the houses.

Once we were taken by car to another home for a party with what the palace called "the VIPs." These men were diplomats and dignitaries from other countries as well as friends of the prince. Upon arrival at the home, we received a tour of the car collections, which were housed in garages made from glass-like showcases. The cars were special, first-off-the-line exotic models. I have since heard that all those cars were left there to rot and rust away because no one took care of them. What a shame!

The palace also had a bowling alley, game rooms, a gymnasium, and much more. On certain occasions when Prince Jefri had a badminton match, we were directed into the auditorium to watch him play.

The kids had fancy custom Mercedes golf carts, and there were times during the day when a few girls would be invited to the polo field to watch the young princes (Prince Jefri's sons) play polo or jet ski at a lake.

Women who were there during their birthdays or a holiday such as Chinese New Year would receive an extra treat in the form of jewelry. In fact, jewelry flowed like water from a faucet. I lived with a jeweler for many years, so I know jewelry, but some of the pieces I saw handed out were incredible. For instance, my friend was one of the prince's girlfriends for a while, and she received a Rolex watch. It came in a huge jewelry box and had solitaire one-carat diamonds the entire way around the band—perhaps a dozen or so—along with more diamonds on the face and bezel. Sometimes, they would hand out incredible jewelry suites, consisting of matching diamond necklaces, earrings, rings, and a bracelet from Bulgari, Cartier, Asprey, and more. And sometimes it was just a plain old diamond Cartier Panthère watch! Not too shabby by any means.

It was like being on *Oprah* or *Ellen...and you get a gift, and you get a gift!* If it was another girl's birthday and you happened to fly in with her, well, guess what? *You get a gift, too!*

At the end of the stay, we were paid in Sing currency that we could exchange for our home country currency before leaving or once we returned to the States.

Now, there were some girls who did get approached for sexual relationships, regardless of what we were told in advance. Some didn't mind being with the prince or his associates.

About the second week of being there, I was asked by one of the Prince's right-hand guys if I would like to be with the doctor of the prince. He was a tall man, well-built, and Middle-Eastern-looking, with the reputation around the parties as being very well endowed.

The doctor? No, thank you. I was told before I left I would not be approached. In fact, I had also been told it would be rude if one of the prince's associates asked for one of the girls, and of course as my luck would have it, I got asked. But I simply said *NO.*

Some of the other girls told me if I didn't go, I'd get sent back. That was no big deal to me. *I'm not compromising myself or selling my soul.*

In the end, though, I was not sent home. I was paid the same amount, and I received a gift of jewelry for my birthday and Chinese New Year.

Because my girlfriend was close with the prince as well as his children, she went back and forth numerous times. And yes, she made bank.

Many girls made boatloads of money—some stayed for many months at a time. Some ended up being hired by the palace and didn't leave for two years. One girl got hit in the head with a polo mallet and ended up in the hospital. They gave her a few million bucks, believe it or not.

Girls were coming back to LA buying homes and businesses. One of Jefri's girlfriends was on the payroll long after she left the prince, and remained so for many years, until she was finally cut off.

I've even heard of celebrities who went there before they became famous, while other celebrities went for special events or parties.

BRUNEI (YES, AGAIN!)

A few months after I returned to the States, my girlfriend said I should go back to Brunei with her. She was going all the time because she was close with the family, especially the young sons.

So I went to meet with the woman who arranged my trip the first time.

She said, "Listen, because you said you wouldn't go with one of the guys from the palace, I'm not sure if I can get you back there so soon. We might need to wait a little longer." *Mmmmmm, really? But I was told I wouldn't even be approached.*

Incognito in Brunei.

I told her I could dye my hair another color. So I put on a wig and met with her just to show her what I would look like. When I walked into the café for our meeting she didn't even recognize me. She said, "Okay, get ready—you're going in two weeks."

So I cut and dyed my hair from blonde to dark brown. Then I changed my eye color and made them a little greener with contact lenses, and off I went.

When someone asked my name, I used my middle name and made up a fake last name. And of course, wouldn't you know it, after being there a week, one of the guys sitting at the party with the doctor said to me, "Oh, you know who you look like? You look just like that girl from *Playboy*—Michele Smith."

I responded, "Oh, gosh, I know her. She's such a bitch. Don't compare me to her!" Somehow, I was able to stay incognito for all the time I was there, which lasted two months. The doctor seemed confused, staring at me intently all the time, trying so hard to figure it out.

My friend and I were asked to stay longer because Prince Hakeem's twenty-first birthday was coming up, and he personally asked us if we minded staying to celebrate. Of course we agreed, though we were a bit disappointed that we wouldn't be going home yet. It was luxurious, yes, but it was also so boring. And for me, it wasn't enough. Sitting around doing nothing is not who I am.

The night of Prince Hakeem's birthday, we were taken down to another palace and put in one of the homes. We had to watch the party from that location. We couldn't actually attend, due to the wife—or should I say, *wives*—of the prince. So we watched from afar and listened to the music.

The musical entertainment was Brian Adams, and I also remember Bobby Brown, Barry White, and Elton John. Joe Montana had tossed a football around on the polo field earlier in the day. I heard that Prince Hakeem wanted to learn how to play American football, so the royal family paid Montana to teach him the game.

The young prince also wished to play the drums with Elton John, so he did on his birthday.

Later that night, when the party was over, all the other girls were chauffeured back to the houses, but my friend and I got called into an office in Prince Hakeem's house. We were told he needed to speak to both of us. We looked at each other as we sat in the room asking, "Why are we here? What did we do? Oh my gosh, what is this all about?" Two hours must have passed. We were tired and planning on flying back to the States the next day.

We waited and waited and waited, until finally "Mike"—as Prince Hakeem liked to be called—walked into the room. I was shaking thinking, *Oh no, this is it, what will I say?* And then he spoke in his nice voice and said, "I want to tell you girls thank you so much for staying for my birthday. I'm very happy that you stayed, and I want to give you a gift." He handed each of us a black linen box signed by Elton John "to Prince Hakeem on his 21st Birthday." When I opened it, there was a CD, a photo of Elton with the prince, and a videotape of the concert. Relieved? Yes, very!

We were told that very few of those boxes were given out. I don't know how many, but I still have mine.

But this story doesn't stop here! After I returned to the States, only a month or two later, I was walking out of the printers on Wilshire Boulevard in LA, and who do you think I ran into? The doctor from Brunei!

I'd heard he had a place in Los Angeles, and it wouldn't have been a big problem running into him, except for the fact that I now had blonde hair, which was still short from my recent trip. So I wasn't exactly sure if he thought I was Michele or that other girl I had pretended to be.

He introduced me to the man he was with, and then he said, "And you are?" *Shit, BUSTED!* I said, "Hi, I'm Michele." He had a very confused look on his face. I guess he was thinking I was the other girl, but my name just came out—I didn't know what to say.

Needless to say, I never went back to Brunei. Not long after, the whole scene fell apart anyway. Many years later, I heard that Prince Jefri was on the run from the sultan, having been accused of mishandling the fortune and spending billions of dollars. I can see why. They auctioned off many of the items from the palace, right down to the light fixtures.

For years, women who went to Brunei were told never to speak about it. We heard we might even be killed if we let the cat out of the bag. But it's been years since I was there, and the story about Prince Jefri mishandling the fortune and having girls at the palace came out sometime in 2010. So I think I'm safe now. I didn't break the news; it was already news!

I did hear of one girl who wrote a book about her experience, and a beauty queen spoke out about her experience as well. She didn't have anything good to say about her time there, so I'm not sure what happened but—I cannot speak for her. I can only tell you my story.

My time there was a special and interesting experience, and as I continue to say, *life is all about experiencing as much as we can.*

This is the first time I have told my story. I did not have a bad experience. There are many people who will frown on this story, and most people would say I was part of a harem, but I don't care. I didn't sell my soul to be "part of the club," as one girl put it when she threw herself at Prince Jefri because some of her friends had already been with him. Afterward, even though she'd approached the prince rather than the other way around, she announced proudly, "I'm a member of the club!"

People have told me I was crazy for not going with the doctor because I could have made a lot of money. I could also make a lot of money doing something else. I think we are all meant to experience whatever life has to offer, but I know where I draw my line.

The funny thing is, I know a girl who did go with that doctor after I refused. She continued to return to Brunei many times. She ended up leaving LA, and I'm pretty sure she retired.

WORKING IN LA

Over the years of my career, I worked on numerous projects. I had small parts on shows like *Married...with Children*, *Full House*, *90210*, *Anything but Love*, and *Out of This World*, just to name a few.

Then there were the commercials for Miller Lite, 7UP, Suzuki, Starburst, and Twizzlers, as well as many more print ads, calendars, and pinup posters. I even did billboards for West Cigarettes in Germany. I had my B films in Indonesia and Argentina, and I worked on bigger projects in the US with small parts.

I appeared in *Playboy* magazine pictorials as well as numerous times in Playboy's *Book of Lingerie* and Playboy's *Bathing Beauties*. I was on two *Playboy* covers, in February '89 and the Japanese issue in September '89. I was also on the covers of *Swimsuit USA*, *Swimwear USA*, and *Muscle & Fitness Magazine* with Lou Ferrigno. It was kind of funny to see myself on the rack in the grocery store while checking out. I even made the *National Enquirer*. ***Because inquiring minds wanna know!***

If you ever walked into a Spencer's Gifts in the '80s or early '90s, you might have found me on playing cards, posters, coffee mugs, postcards, and even wrapping paper. Yep, I did pretty much everything because I enjoyed it—and it paid the bills.

To this day, there are things that pop up now and then. Someone will ask me if I was in a production, and it will jog my memory. I'll say, "Oh, yeah, I think I was in that." It seems like such a long time ago, and it's hard to remember every project I worked on, but I can remember some gigs very well, right down to what I was wearing on set that day.

Working as a model and actress in Los Angeles, I kept wondering: ***What will I do when I get older? When will this all end?*** Because as most people know, when a woman ages in Hollywood, the parts become few and far between. I was always thinking of other ideas—looking out through the windshield and not in the rearview!

So in the late '90s, I decided to open a small model and talent agency with my former booker from Playboy, Danice. We called it Sunset West, and we were in a high-rise building right on the corner of Sunset and La Cienega. We did the best we could, but there was a lot of competition with agencies back then. Getting bigger clients was harder than we'd imagined. The one thing that I did get out of it was a booking for a TV show called *American Thunder*.

We closed the agency after three years, but I kept hosting the show.

PART IV

American Thunder

So You Know…

SO…I TURNED THIRTY-EIGHT! I CELEBRATED MY BIRTHDAY with friends at a local restaurant in LA. Of course, there was plenty of champagne, since I didn't know whether that would indeed be my last year. The worry wasn't something I ever mentioned to anyone, but I could certainly celebrate with the best of them. So I turned thirty-eight and waited.

But I didn't sit still to wait! This was the busiest point in my life. I had a very successful hosting gig on *American Thunder*, and at the same time designed and patented Jeweled G's G-strings. I have always loved being busy, and I had a double whammy with the TV show and being a lingerie designer. I enjoyed every minute of it.

At motorcycle events, guys would often say to me, "This has got to be a dream job for you!" Riding a bike and getting paid for it? Hosting *American Thunder* sure was a dream job. But, just to be on the safe side, I said my Biker Prayer every single time I threw my leg over a motorcycle, and I still do today if I go out for a ride.

During the years of doing *American Thunder*, I learned how most of the fans appreciated and loved me—something I never could have imagined. Owners of motorcycle shops came up to me, saying, "Thank you for what you have done for the motorcycle industry. You have changed things for us in regard to more women riding." It took me years to realize that maybe I did do something for that industry.

But the important thing is, I never let it get to my head. When you are any kind of celebrity in a business where you have people watching you, it's important to keep your feet on the ground. Motorcycle enthusiasts from all walks of life came to see me—guys who barely had enough gas in their tank to get to an event. I valued all the fans and enjoyed our interactions. My appreciation for them was real, after they'd tuned in every Tuesday night for so many years.

The years of success built my confidence, but there was still something more I needed. I didn't in any way want to slow down. If anything, I just wanted to move faster.

AMERICAN THUNDER

In the late 1990s, I did a photo shoot for a biker clothing catalog in Idyllwild, California, put out by *Easyriders Magazine* and featuring riding clothes for both men and women. When the catalog came out, I ended up on the cover, sitting on a motorcycle. The name of that catalog was *Roadware*.

The producer from WATV spotted me on the cover, tracked me down, called Danice at Sunset West, and asked, "Can she actually ride a motorcycle?" Lucky for me, I had recently obtained my motorcycle (MC) license and taken the motorcycle safety course.

At that time in Los Angeles, it seemed like every other

commercial audition I went on, I was asked if I could ride a motorcycle. Before taking the course, I'd had a role in a French film, but they hired a body double for me to do the riding. I was so mortified when I had to sit on a motorcycle in the back of a pickup truck and ride down Hollywood Boulevard for the close-up shots. Then, when they brought in the body double to do the riding, she was about ninety pounds soaking wet on a freaking phone book. I thought to myself, *If this girl can hold up an 800 pound Harley, so can I.* So off I went to MC school. The timing was perfect!

American Thunder years. Photo: Marcel Indik Photography.

After confirming with Danice that yes, I really could ride a motorcycle, I was called into the studio to read for this cable motorcycle TV show called *American Thunder*.

I ended up booking the gig for very little money, but in LA at that time, a gig was a gig, so I took the job. It truly didn't pay much at all in the beginning, but I didn't care because it meant exposure and a year's contract.

Getting a year-long contract as an actress, model, and TV host in LA was a good thing. It meant I didn't have to pound the pavement for castings as much as before.

And you wanna know what the best part of that one-year gig was? It actually turned into an eleven-year gig! I had a good long run on that show and made a name for myself in the motorcycle industry amongst the Harley-Davidson/V-twin riders, both male and female. *American Thunder* turned out to be one of the longest-running motorcycle shows on TV.

The rest is history.

THE *AMERICAN THUNDER* YEARS

I'm not gonna say the early years were easy working in a male dominated industry, but the show kept building viewership, and I had more fans each year.

The guys would gather together in their garages—or as they called them, "man caves"—to watch *American Thunder* every Tuesday night on Speed Channel. It aired again every Saturday morning, and then on Thanksgiving, there was an all-day *American Thunder* marathon.

It took a few years to get some of the builders on my side, or at least that's what it felt like. I think there were a few in the industry who wanted to know why I got that hosting gig when I didn't grow up riding bikes. But hey, it was what it was, and I just so happened to book it and keep it longer than the other two hosts had previously—one being Michael Madsen, who went on to do bigger and better things, and the other being Chad McQueen. The show just didn't seem to work with a male host.

After years of hosting, I became a fixture in the industry and gained much more acceptance. People called me an American motorcycle icon, the first lady of motorcycling, motorcycle ambassador, and a few other things.

Because of the show, I began to get called for personal appearances around the country. I'd go meet and greet motorcycle enthusiasts, take photos, participate in charity rides, and sign autographs.

A lot of the show segments were shot in the studio using a teleprompter, while others were shot in different locations around Los Angeles. But the most fun for me was going on the road, literally traveling in fast-forward, to events like Sturgis, South Dakota, and Daytona Bike Week, as well as shooting in Hawaii—what fun!

One of my charity rides.

I had a great time doing our segment called "Man on the Street," where I would interview fans randomly. That was the best part of the job for me—interacting with all of those people who tuned in every week to watch *American Thunder*. That show ended for me in 2009, and I went on to do another show called *Two Wheel Thunder* with the same producers, but it only lasted one season.

I continued doing personal appearances for about seven years after the show ended and had a line of motorcycle merchandise as well. I had great times and some crazy times at many motorcycle events. I rode on the beach in Daytona, on the streets of Mexico, and in the winding hills of Hawaii and Sturgis, South Dakota. I did charity rides and motorcycle events from Colorado Springs, Colorado, to Philadelphia, and everywhere in between. I had the privilege of riding with the Blue Knights in New York City as well as firefighters in the Carolinas and up in Wisconsin. Oh yeah, and then there was the guy who always showed up at events with the jars of moonshine cherries. *Yum!* Hey, everyone needs a little zing in their zang!

I had a guy who tattooed my photograph on his leg at a motorcycle event in Daytona—I wonder if his girlfriend or wife made him cover it up, *LOL.* There was the guy who sent me his mother's diamond wedding rings and said I should have them. I asked him to send me his return address so I could ship them back, and I did. Everyone brought me gifts at the personal appearances, including children.

Once a small boy about six years old showed up wearing a T-shirt that said, "I love Michele Smith," and holding a bouquet of roses. Then there was the guy on his way to Daytona with a sign tied to the back of his pickup that said, "In search of Michele Smith." There were lines of people at the meet and greets, and I always did my best never to cut off the line. I stayed until everyone had a chance to have a photo or a chat. One of my first appearances was in Carlisle, Pennsylvania, not far from where I grew up. I often had my little sister with me to help out. As they drove us up to the event building, I said to my sister, "Wow, I wonder who that line is for?" Turned out it was for me! Gosh, I couldn't believe it. And yes, I was happy to have so many admirers.

Some people just wanted to ask me questions, and others had bike tales to tell me or photos of a bike they'd just built. Women told me if not for watching my show, they would have never had the courage to ride a motorcycle. Men told me they were laid up in the hospital from an accident, and the only thing that got them through it was hearing my voice each week on *American Thunder*. There were dealership owners who said, "I do believe my sales to women went up because of you."

Many people said thank you for what I'd done in the motorcycle community, but it took me years to let that gratitude fully sink in and believe I'd contributed. I also managed to keep both feet on the ground, and sometimes talking about all of it isn't easy—but I'm writing a book, so I have to tell the story.

I'm proud to have been a part of the motorcycle culture.

After all, these were the people who supported the show by tuning in each week, and I appreciated them.

Some guys would ride five hours just to say hello, even though they may have seen me at an event the month before. (It gave them an excuse to get out and ride.) They would come up and say hi, take a photo, hop back on the bike, and ride the five hours back home. Then there was the guy who came every year to an event and stayed in a hotel for the weekend, hanging out at my booth and hoping I might go to dinner with him.

A guy once showed up at an event in Pennsylvania and asked me if I would come out into the parking lot to talk to him. I looked at him kind of funny because he was wearing a turtle-neck, and most bikers don't wear turtlenecks, especially in warm weather. He creeped me out. I said, "Whatever you want to talk to me about, you can just do it right here." He asked me if I would go out that evening to dinner with him. I said, "I'm sorry but I have to fly out right after this for another appearance, but I do appreciate the offer." He replied in a loud and irate voice, "I just drove six hours"—he didn't have a MC—"to come see you. The least you could do is get in the car with me and go have dinner." I was thinking, *Yeah, right, where is he going to put me—in the trunk?*

And some crazy guy—I think he was an inmate from some-where in the South—wrote a ten-page letter telling me how he was going to take me to a motel when he got out of jail, and proceeded to get a little more explicit—more than I needed to hear. Letters like that I just put in what I call the "kook" file.

I know some of you might be reading this and saying, "Oh, those mean old bikers," when in fact, it's quite the opposite. I have worked in three male-dominated industries so far in my life: motorcycling, *Playboy*, and horse racing. I can tell you motorcycle enthusiasts—or "big bad bikers," as some people think they are—whether an average biker or a motorcycle club member, have all been very respectful toward me. Bikers are always the first to show up when you need to raise money for charity. If a fellow biker is stranded on the road, they will always stop to help. They are good people, and I will always have great respect for the motorcycle community.

The only regret I had working on *American Thunder* is that I didn't get the opportunity to let the fans know that the show would be changing its format. The show executives called me less than two weeks before the new season was about to start and said they'd decided not to have a regular host. They would be bringing in the guy who won the first year of the TV show *Survivor* (Colby) and two young girls who didn't ride. They wanted me to do a small cameo part in a show I'd carried all those years. We couldn't agree on the money, and in the end, I basically said, "Go on without me and see how it works out for you." They did, and the fans complained. They actually started a blog with thousands of complaints and requests to "bring back Michele." *American Thunder* ended up getting canceled that year after just a few episodes.

I always said if they just would have let me tape an episode that explained the changes to the viewers, the show would have had a chance to continue. Goes to show you *if it ain't broke, don't fix it.* I hated leaving my viewers hanging. They were my fans, my people, my friends—but my hands were tied. And as they say, that's show biz. But sometimes, show biz really sucks!

BE SEXY, BE EDIBLE, BEJEWELED

In early 2000, when low-rise jeans became a thing and women everywhere (especially in LA) were running around with their ass cracks showing, I had an idea!

I would see women bending over with plumber's crack, some who had tattoos on their lower back, others who had nothing but a piece of fabric sticking out of their jeans. At the time, I had just started the online gemologist course with the Gemological Institute of America (GIA), and I came up with this idea to make a jeweled G-string that I called Jeweled G's.

Because I wanted to patent it, I had to find a way to make it harder to knock off, which meant going beyond just a design patent. I went for a utility patent on a G-string that...*wait for it*...turned into a necklace! Yes, I made it so the jewelry actually detached from the panty, allowing you to wash the garment without ruining the jewelry and to wear the jewelry around your neck. *Ha ha ha.* Sounds kinky, I know, but it really wasn't.

Decorating derrieres everywhere with my Jeweled G's. Photo: Marcel Indik Photography.

The lawyer I had hired to help me dropped the ball on maintaining my patent, and he let it go into abandonment. I guess he thought it wasn't important enough, so I fought for it myself. I was constantly calling the patent office and taking down notes regarding whom I talked to and what was said. And finally I got it—a great accomplishment, I think, and I didn't need a college education for that one!

It took me two years to get that patent and a lot of money. In the end when the lawyer sent me his bill for all of his "hard" work, I replied with my notes on all the legwork I'd done and told him, "I think you need to rethink the amount I owe you." And he did just that.

So I hold a patent on a G-string called Jeweled G's. (Well, it's actually patented as jewelry, hence the utility patent.) Now, I can't say I created or invented something that saved lives, but I may have saved some sex lives.

I was a one-woman show—sewing, beading, running around all over downtown and East LA to gather my materials. I would then take my finished product to stores and boutiques as well as Las Vegas casinos. Eventually, I was able to get the product into Victoria's Secret. I ended up in 160 Victoria's Secret stores across the country as well as in their catalog. In fact, at one point I became so busy with the G-strings that I almost quit my TV show.

Victoria's Secret approved an overseas factory, so eventually I was able to make the product without doing all the work myself. The process consisted of two parts: the fabric in one country and the beaded jeweled piece in another, so it would not be knocked off before I had it in the stores. Victoria's Secret also made the G-strings pass what was called a thirteen-pound "grab force test," which basically meant they put it on a machine and stretched it to see at what point it might break. Who knew a G-string could be so complicated?

Once I had both product pieces, my friends helped with

assembling the products, then bagging and tagging them for Victoria's Secret. It was a fun time, and I enjoyed the experience. *Great conversation starter as well!*

Because I was working with a PR agency, I had articles written in magazines about the product, and twice they appeared in the "Potpourri" section of *Playboy*—once with the Jeweled G's and another time with the Edible G's. I couldn't believe the response and the orders that came flowing in after the coverage.

About the edibles: the Edible Sweet G's were created as just another fun product to add to the G-string collection I already had going. The Jeweled G's were a great product, but I wanted to find something that I could make an edible G-string out of. The first thing that came to mind was those little pastel candy necklaces most of us had as kids. So I made a few samples using the candy necklaces, and it took off from there. They ended up in *Playboy*, and I offered them in various boutiques in Las Vegas. The Palms Hotel had a fairly nice display in their window of a cigar girl mannequin holding a tray of my edible sweet G's.

I even made refills for the panty once the candy was gone.

I once took a bag filled with G-strings to the South of France. I went from boutique to boutique, showing my goods. But the shop that stands out the most was a small one in Juan-les-Pins. The owner just loved what she called "the bonbons" (candies)!

That nice French lady must have phoned me a million times that year—she was constantly ordering "the bonbons"! The sales paid for my holiday that summer to the South of France.

Another time, The Dutchman called me from Amsterdam. He said, "Hey, I have a girl here who wants to order your G-strings. Can you bring some to Amsterdam?" Off I went with about 300 strings in my bag.

I was "decorating derrières" all over the US and in Europe! Once a friend of mine who is a registered nurse (RN) took a bunch with her to the Middle East. She told me that although the women must stay covered up, they still love to wear sexy lingerie. So while she was there administering Botox and fillers in private homes, she was also selling the Jeweled G's. Ladies were swinging from the chandeliers everywhere!

Because I spent a lot of money to get a patent, I was very protective of my creation. Lingerie and fashion people can be ruthless! I had heard there was a lady in Léon, France, who, via my middleman in Beverly Hills, was trying to knock off my G-strings. I flew over to France to the lingerie show and scoped out her display. I'm pretty sure my middleman tipped her off in advance. I think he was trying to get a deal going with her for Europe. I didn't see an exact copy of my Jeweled G's, but she did have the edibles, which I didn't have a patent on.

I decided to take my G-strings to an erotica show at the LA Convention Center one year. I had never attended an erotica show before, and I must say, it was quite fun. I had a small setup right next to the nipple rings, and across from me was a product called The Pussy Shaver! What fun it was to watch all the action.

I had a good laugh when a few guys asked me which porno video was I in—and when another one said, "Excuse me, do you swing?" I answered, "Why yes, I do—at the park!" *LMAO!* I actually picked up one of my biggest clients at that event: the Hard Rock Casino in Las Vegas.

One time, I pulled the wrong suitcase off the belt while flying into an airport in Pennsylvania. I had just left a convention and G-strings were spread out on a display board in my bag. I threw the suitcase in the car and went on to the next destination. A few hours later, I received a phone call from Delta asking if I could please check the bag I'd picked up. The representative said, "We think you have a gentleman's bag because he has a bag with your name on it."

To my surprise, when I opened the suitcase, it was filled with men's clothes—which meant his suitcase was filled with tiny pearl and gemstone G-strings. *Oops, my bad. But oh, how I wish I would have been there to see the look on his face when he opened the bag...better yet, what if his wife unpacked it?*

Jeweled G's kept me going for many years after the initial hype wore off, and I miss the days of inventing and creating such an entertaining product!

BIKER STORIES

With Sickboy Motorcycles at OC Bikefest.

From the late '90s up until 2010, I was filming *American Thunder*. Most weekends, you could find me at a bike event somewhere across the country. When I wrapped both of the shows, I spent another seven years making the rounds with personal appearances and selling my line of motorcycle wear.

Writing a book was the furthest thing from my mind. But after thinking about the way a lot of my life had gone, I decided to go forward with this book and felt the need to include selected stories and experiences that I had within the motorcycle community. After all, bikers have been a huge part of my life for many years. And although I took a much needed break from social media, I wanted to come back and include some of the fine people of motorcycling in this memoir. Here are some of my stories...

Disclaimer: I am not part of, nor do I support, any motorcycle club or people/persons affiliated with such. I have great respect for all of my fellow bikers and am simply telling the stories as they happened to me.

JAY LENO, LOVE RIDE, LOS ANGELES

Jay Leno's interview was one of the hardest I had to do. It was during the Love Ride in Los Angeles, a thirty-five-mile charity motorcycle ride that was held yearly in Southern California. It was the largest one-day fundraising motorcycle event in the world and always a lot of fun. The ride started in Glendale and ended up at Castaic Lake with music and a barbecue. I had actually participated in the Love Ride before I became the host of *American Thunder*. It was my very first charity ride.

There was nothing better than being in the middle of a sea of bikes and hearing the sounds of the motors revving up, especially that famous Harley sound: "potato...potato ...potato..." It was such a rush.

Jay Leno was the grand marshal for the event.

We had finished all of our shooting for the morning, and the bikers were getting the bikes revved up and raring to go. We waited and waited for Jay to show up. I had just packed up and was ready to take off, when I heard the crew say, "Here comes Jay Leno." All the news crews started running for him, and so did I!

I somehow managed to shove the microphone into the circle of the news people and asked, "Hey, Jay, what did you ride in on this morning?" I hoped he would tell me about his Harley or whatever it was, but he just gave me a very simple, smart-ass answer in his signature way: "A bike, what do you think?" All I could do was laugh! I was not well-seasoned with my hosting gig yet, and I just went with it, saying, "Thanks, Jay!"

SONNY BARGER, HELLS ANGEL CHAPTER FOUNDING MEMBER, OAKLAND, CALIFORNIA

I'll never forget what the producer said to me on *American Thunder* when I was waiting to do an interview with Sonny Barger in early 2000. We were in a small motorcycle museum in Sturgis, South Dakota. He explained to me how Sonny, who started the Oakland, California, chapter of the Hells Angels had just gotten back from a "vacation." He said, "But whatever you do, don't ask him where he was."

"Okay," I said, "I get it." His vacation was obviously someplace behind bars.

BIG RED ENGINE, SOUTH FLORIDA

In early 2000, I was in Florida, working on my house. I threw on a T-shirt to run out for some coffee early one morning, without thinking too much about what I was wearing. I have tons of motorcycle tees, most of which were given to me over the years by people in the business who wanted to advertise a product. The shirt I put on this particular day said "Big Red Engine." I had even worn it once on an episode of *American Thunder*.

The Big Red Engine is a brand used by the Hells Angels to promote the products they sell to the public.

So there I was, standing in a line inside Panera Bread, waiting to order my morning coffee. Two biker guys were in line, talking quietly and looking at me, but I couldn't tell what they were saying.

Finally, they said, "Hey, excuse me, but you can't wear that T-shirt here in Florida."

What?

They said, "This is Outlaw territory, and you're wearing a Hells Angel T-shirt." Outlaws and Hells Angels have been rivals for many years.

I said, "I can wear anything I want! Besides, it was given to me by a Hells Angel member in Amsterdam, and it's what I felt like throwing on."

Then they said, "Hey, where do we know you from?"

"I host a TV show called *American Thunder* on Speed Channel," I told them.

They said, "Oh, we are very sorry. We know that show, and you can wear anything you want."

Lol...you're damn right I can.

NO NEEDLES TATTOO

When I was at the prime of hosting my TV show, which would have been the early to mid-2000s, I got a pretty significant amount of email on a daily basis. Every morning, I'd go through the list and answer all my fan mail myself.

My fans would ask all sorts of questions about the show. They might ask about something they saw on an episode, such as a certain helmet I was wearing, or where my next appearance would be. A lot of the time, women asked about an article of clothing I wore on one of the episodes.

But I found one particular email rather amusing. This viewer was very mad at me. He said, "My daughter watches you every week, and she looks up to you as a role model and as a woman riding a motorcycle." He went on about how he was upset that I went out and ruined my skin with all those tattoos. "I can't believe you would do that," he said, and he went on and on and on.

No Needles Tattoo! Photo: Marcel Indik Photography.

I couldn't take it anymore, I had to answer his email first thing. So very politely, I told how I just came out with a new line of T-shirts called No Needles Tattoo. They had fake nylon tattoo sleeves attached, and they looked just like the real deal. I said, "Don't worry, I didn't get my arms tattooed."

He said, "Oh my gosh, I am so sorry!"

I'm not sure, but he may have even ordered one after that.

The tattoo shirts really made an impression with people, but not always in a positive way. I found it fascinating how people can be so quick to judge another person just because they are inked.

Does having a portrait or words inked on your skin make you a terrible person? I don't think so, but to each his own, I suppose.

One time after I finished one of my personal appearances, I had to run to catch my flight back to LA. I had no time to change clothes, and I just so happened to be wearing one of my No Needles Tattoo shirts. As I walked into the boarding area and sat down, two elderly people next to me actually got up and moved down a few seats, giving me an odd look. I guess I was too freaky for them. *Ohhhh, those big bad biker tattoos.*

After about five minutes of sitting there, I casually leaned back in the seat and decided to push up my tattoo sleeves. The look on their faces was priceless. And I kid you not: they moved back to their original seats next to me.

A HUG GOES A LONG WAY

Over the years, fellow bikers, vendors, and MC business owners have given me all sorts of gifts and swag. I've received T-shirts, leather jackets, a sink faucet that looks like a motorcycle tank, drumsticks from a biker band that used to play at one of my events, parts and accessories with bling, a beautiful hand-tooled leather motorcycle seat, a piece of rock that came out of some mine in Colorado that was engraved "Miners dig Michele," and many more too numerous to mention.

I must have also given and received thousands of hugs while working out in the field. One of the things I always liked to do was surprise the fans by doing something nice. For me, a handshake was never enough. I found it humorous when they would put out their hand for a shake and say, "Hello, Miss Smith." Miss Smith? I'd say, "Just call me Michele." I know they were all being respectful and polite, but I just couldn't help myself. I would put my arms out and say, "Oh, c'mon, give me a hug."

After a few years, most of them knew the deal. They would still ask for a handshake but wait for the hug. And sometimes I would get that really sweaty gross biker hug—the kind where a big guy wearing a sleeveless shirt puts his arms around you, his sweaty armpits end up on your shoulders, and when he walks away, the sweat remains...the things I did for my fans.

But hey, these were my people—my supporters, my friends, or shall I say, "frans."

Other times, someone would tell me a friend had wanted to come out to the event, but that person was in the hospital, had to work, or just couldn't make the ride. I would say, "Why don't we call him?" Their eyes would get big with excitement, and they'd say, "Really?" Most of the time, the person I called didn't believe it was really me. It was all in good fun, and I loved making someone's day.

WOMEN BIKERS

I had almost as many female motorcycle enthusiasts as male. In the beginning, I had a sense that most women were not sure what to think. Here was this female TV host hugging their biker guys (though, by the way, I always asked for permission if a lady was present). But I talked to everyone. I was just as interested in hearing their stories as they were in hearing mine.

Women would tell me how they never thought they could ride a bike until they watched my show. Then they thought, *why not?* And that's exactly right: ***why the hell not?*** I always suggested they take a motorcycle safety course first, as some women complained that their partners just didn't have patience when trying to teach them.

Once you take a course, you get the hang of it pretty quick. There were a few women who fell over or went straight into a canal. In their cases, I'd suggest, "Why don't you stick to being a passenger on the bike with your man? After all, you get to wrap your arms around him while you're riding." (Plus, it's safer for all of us.)

I had numerous conversations and took many photos over the years with female riders. In the end, it was usually the women looking for me, even more than the men.

And then there were the women who would find me at an event for their husband and say, "Honey, your girlfriend is here!" Or if they saw me on TV, it was, "Honey, your girlfriend's on TV." I have always appreciated the support from my female fans. ***Thanks, ladies.***

WALL OF DEATH RIDERS

When you're out doing personal appearances at motorcycle events, you often run into the same people. It makes sense; we are all in the same business. A lot of the time, we'll say, "Hey, see you at the next one." So I was used to seeing a lot of the same setups.

A familiar one at the outdoor events was The Wall of Death.

If you don't know what that is, I suggest you search for "Wall of Death motorcycle riders" on YouTube. The video speaks for itself.

They are amazing and highly skilled at what they do. And believe me, you must be skilled, because one wrong move, and you could be toast!

I have seen both men and women riders do this stunt: they ride on a motorcycle around the vertical wall of a huge stage like a wooden barrel, defying gravity and being held in place by centrifugal force! They finally make their way to the top, where the spectators are watching, and they grab money from the hands of the spectators for the performance.

It has been referred to as a carnival sideshow. I'm sorry, but I think it's much more than that. In my eyes, it's beautiful to watch and not just a special skill but an art form. Although some say it's just plain crazy, I think these riders deserve much more credit than they receive.

I have seen the Wall of Death in Daytona, Myrtle Beach, and Sturgis. It's exciting and mesmerizing to watch these riders going round and round. Honestly, it's tough to comprehend how the hell they do that. But every time I see it, it's like I'm watching it for the first time.

PLEASE...DON'T FORGET TO PUT YOUR FEET DOWN

I'm not really sure why bikers, babes, and beer always go together. I mean, that's how most of the events are advertised. Well, okay, I guess I get the "babes" part of it, but combining beer and riding just doesn't seem to be such a smart idea.

Almost every event serves beer. It's everywhere. It's biker fuel, and it's how you get the riders to attend in the first place— throw in some music and you got it made.

Personally, I can't throw back a pint and then toss my leg over a bike. Call me a lightweight, a wimp, or whatever it may be, but I don't want to take the chance.

But it happens all the time. Bikers drink and ride. Not everyone is a lightweight. And yes, sometimes there are accidents and sometimes not.

One of the more gruff bikers I met at an event in Vegas told me the story of how he got shit-faced drunk late at night, "wasted," as he put it, and just had to get home. He fired up his bike and off he went, hoping to make it home safe. He said at every red light and stop sign, he'd fall over: "I forgot to put my feet down!"

All I could think was, *At least he stopped.* And *if only I could have seen that on video.* "Once I got home, I couldn't figure out how to put the kickstand down to stand up the bike," he said, so "I just laid it down on its side…like it was going to sleep."

I consider him one lucky dude.

IS IT A MOTOR*CYCLE* OR A MOTOR "SICKLE?"

I've mentioned I'm highly attracted to accents, mostly accents of the foreign kind—but hey, I love hearing accents from all walks of life!

On one episode of *American Thunder*, I interviewed a guy who owned a transport company. He picked up the bikes and drove them to their final destination, in situations when someone purchased a new bike or wanted to attend a bike week but didn't have time to ride the whole way there.

As this guy proceeded to tell me about his business, he said "motor sickle" over and over again. I loved listening to him speak. It was like that Arlo Guthrie song when he says, "I just wanna ride my motor sickle."

The transport company owner reminded me of the guys who came out to see me at a personal appearance and take a photo. They'd hand the camera to a friend and say, "Mash the button!" That translates to: push the button. And as they were mashing the button, they would tell me how "purdy" I am! *Gotta love those Southern accents, and especially all the motor "sickles"!*

YOU AUTOGRAPHED A *WHAT?*

Over the years, I've been asked to autograph just about everything. *Yes, I said "just about."* But I have been asked over and over again to autograph bald heads. I'm not sure why, but it seemed to be the second most popular request after autographing photos.

I mean, c'mon, why just get a photo autographed when you can get your bald head autographed? And I didn't mind doing it. To me, it was all in good fun. If they asked, then I was happy to do it. I never charged for an autograph. Sometimes I sold posters, but I always had pics to give away, and if anyone brought something for me to sign, I did so with pleasure.

Guys would say, "Hey, Michele! Do you think you could come out to the parking lot and autograph my tank?" I would say, "Sure." Later on, they would clear coat it to make it last longer.

I signed jeans, casts, leather vests, jackets, patches, boots, saddle bags, helmets, arms, backs, legs, heads, chests, and not one but *two* prosthetic legs...just about *everything.* Of course, I did have to draw the line somewhere. Sometimes they wanted the signature to tattoo over, and other times they wanted it just for kicks. Some even did it to piss off their girlfriend, to which I would say, "Please don't tell her where I'm set up."

The worst part about signing a bald head was the fact that afterward, I had to toss the Sharpie. Too much oil. I know, *gross,* but hey, you just have to go with the flow!

Sometimes guys would show up with my old *Playboy* magazines or calendars. I once had a guy show up with what must have been thirty different videos from TV shows and whatever else he found me in. But I didn't mind. Whatever they wanted me to sign, I did.

Once, while I was at an event in Arizona, a guy came up to the front of the line with what looked to be just a plain white helmet. He said in a rather soft voice, "Hey, would you please sign this helmet for me?" I asked if he was sure that wouldn't ruin it. He said, "Oh, no, I have only one other signature on this helmet, and I would like to add yours." He went on to tell me how that other signature was from Evel Knievel!

My jaw dropped. I said, "Are you absolutely sure I won't ruin this helmet?" He said, "No way, please sign it," and it was my pleasure!

DON'T MAKE A BUCKET LIST—LIVE YOUR BUCKET LIST

At one of my motorcycle events, someone once asked me if I had a bucket list. I literally didn't know what a bucket list was. After he explained, I thought about it, and *why would anyone make a bucket list? Why wouldn't you just live your bucket list?!*

For most of my life, I have lived every day like it's my last. If there is something I want to see or a place I want to go, I make a point to get there and see it, one way or another.

I took jobs in places because I wanted to see the country and experience the culture. I was lucky enough to be able to do that.

I have never made a bucket list because I lived it!

Pilgrimage

So You Know…

MY MOTHER'S SISTER LUCILLE LIVED IN GREECE MOST OF her life. I hadn't seen her since I was a small child, but she always sent me a card at Christmas with photos as well as a letter here and there. Unlike the rest of my mother's family, Lucille kept in contact with me. So when I finally got to Greece in 2005 to see her, it was exciting. She told me stories about my mother and their other sisters, and we enjoyed our time together.

I went back to Greece three more times to visit her, and I also met her daughter, my cousin. My aunt was a funny, outgoing, lovely person, and I wish I could have spent more time with her. She offered a window into a part of my life that I'd lost, and I loved spending time with her and learning about my mother and their family. She created a memory lane where there hadn't been one before.

And talk about a memory lane—the Camino!

When I walked the Camino in 2019, I was motivated by curiosity. I'd heard it was a very spiritual pilgrimage and walking it cured people of ailments. Pilgrims reportedly came back from the Camino feeling much better than when they left. I wanted to do it—I wanted the experience.

I needed to walk off a lot of sins, and the way I look at it, one mile is worth one sin. That year I walked eighty-three miles in six days. I'll be going back and walking more!

And you know what? A couple of weeks before I left, I had so much pain in my knees that I wasn't sure if I'd be able to do it. But I had already made the commitment, and I wasn't backing out. I have to tell you, by the end, every single pain had gone away, never to return!

I had a very enlightening experience on one of the days there, and I came back refreshed and full of energy. It's amazing what a walk can do for you!

What I learned about myself on all of these adventures is that it's good to experience as much as you can while you're still able to. You have to be able to get up and move and get out and see the world. Don't stop because you'll have plenty of time to rest when you're dead and gone.

So keep moving.

GREECE

Greece was a country I had always wanted to visit. My Aunt Lucille lived there most of her life, and I hadn't seen her since I was a child. In 2005, I decided to take the trip. I flew into Athens and booked a hotel for a few nights so I could visit with my aunt. She was in her eighties but still full of life, and I found her to be very humorous. She took me sightseeing through Athens and showed me all the typical tourist areas, from the Acropolis to the little Greek tavernas in alleyways that I never could have found on my own. The food was amazing.

In Greece with Aunt Lucille.

My aunt told me all about her life in Greece. She had moved there in the '60s and married a Greek man. She had two kids with him and years later divorced. But she never came back to live in the States because the children loved Greece so much. Who could blame them? It is quite a beautiful place.

In the afternoons, I would sit by the hotel pool; later, I'd meet up with Aunt Lucille. It was during one of those poolside afternoons that a local Greek guy spotted me. I must have been in my own world and not noticed him. After returning to my hotel room, there was a knock at my door. I opened it, and there in the doorway was a drop-dead gorgeous man who looked like he had just stepped out of the pages of *GQ*. He was holding a single rose like he'd walked off *The Bachelor*!

His hands were shaking as he said, "Hello, I saw you at the pool today, and I wanted to know if you would have a drink with me?" My first question was how the heck he knew my room number. He said, "The waiter gave it to me."

Great, are you kidding me? So much for security. I thanked him but said I already had plans for the evening, and the next morning I was leaving for Mykonos.

Lucille had told me, "When you come to Greece, you cannot just stay in Athens!" I asked her which of the islands I should visit, and she said, "Mykonos, of course! That's the party island! That's where all the action happens! You have to see Mykonos!"

So off I went to Mykonos! Flying over, I could see all the white houses with beautiful blue-domed roofs. I still remember the feeling I got when I opened the shuttered doors in my room and stepped onto the balcony overlooking the island. *Wow, gorgeous*—and I couldn't wait to explore more.

One night while I was walking through the quaint streets of Mykonos Town, the main town on the island, I came across a store called The Corner Jewelry Shop. I walked inside and immediately started talking with a lady in her seventies. She said, "When you are here on the island of Mykonos, you need to go out to the clubs. And the clubs don't get going until after midnight—way after." I laughed and told her I was there on my own, and she said, "You should meet my son. Come back in half an hour, and I will introduce you." So I did.

I met her very muscular and very Greek Adonis-looking, handsome son, Stathis. We became fast friends and a bit more. He showed me the town and introduced me to all his friends and family. I ended up going back to Mykonos many more times.

Stathis took me to places I would have never seen on my own. He showed me every corner of Mykonos, sometimes from the back of his motorbike. We went to beaches, restaurants, and friends' homes. We watched the belly dancers in the local bars. We ate and drank in the streets of Mykonos, and of course—as his mother suggested—we went out to the clubs late into the night, until the wee hours of the morning. Mykonos was a fabulous place!

On one trip, we spent the weekend high in the mountains in a place called Nafplion. We ate freshly pressed olive oil with the most amazing feta cheese and fresh Greek pita—the best I have ever had. We explored the town's castle and ate in the tavernas.

On another trip, we explored Spetses and Thessaloníki, two places the average person might not choose when visiting Greece. It was a wonderful experience. It's always great when you have a local to show you the places you might not otherwise see.

In the fall, we went back to Athens and had lunch with my aunt. We walked around the city and spent the evenings with his friends in what is called the *bouzoukia,* where you sit around a stage and listen to Greek music and singers while you drink whiskey and toss flowers on the stage. What fun! They once told me that people used to toss plates on the stage, but thankfully that tradition changed years ago.

On another visit, I attended a traditional Greek wedding. It was beautiful! I returned the favor for his hospitality and invited Stathis to visit me in Los Angeles. He stayed with me for two months. We spent Thanksgiving, Christmas, and New Year's together. I showed him all the tourist places in Los Angeles. We also went to Florida, where he visited Disney World for the first time.

I have taken several trips to Greece and cannot say enough about the country, food, scenery, and the Greeks themselves.

Opa!

THAILAND

In February 2006, Stathis invited me to Phuket, Thailand. (No, it is not pronounced "fuck it" as some people say but rather "Pu-ket.")

With my Greek god in Thailand.

Stathis spent a few months of each year in Thailand, and he'd told me how much he loved it because it was so cheap—the hotels, food, even five-dollar massages on the beach. For some reason, Thailand was never a country that was high on my list to visit. But after hearing all of his stories, I thought, *Why not?*

Getting there took two days, so I got a ticket to leave two days before my birthday so that I would actually arrive on my birthday.

Thailand was wonderful—even with the humidity that clings to you as your hair frizzes up and the sweat rolls down your back. It's a hot, lazy, laid-back kind of wonderland. I stayed in the crystal clear water for hours each day and dug my feet into the sand, watching the tiny fish swim around me. I bathed in those waters for two weeks and felt so relaxed every single day. We stayed on the beach all day, every day, having massages and eating food freshly cooked by the locals. At night, we hung out at the local bars where I was mesmerized by watching the kathoeys, or ladyboys as they were called when I was there.

If you don't know what a ladyboy is, they're basically guys who decided to be a lady, or at least half a lady, meaning they've had a boob job but still kept their male lower parts. The definition also includes transvestite or transsexual prostitutes. Whatever the details, it's their choice and they are recognized as a third gender in Thai culture.

And let me tell you something—some of them were beautiful. From their perfectly applied makeup, well-groomed hair, and impeccably manicured nails to the way they walked, talked, and carried themselves. I really could see how some men wouldn't know the difference. *But I always knew.* I loved watching them parade around, some like a proud peacock, others more shy. I found them intriguing. I could sit and watch their mannerisms for hours. There was also a cabaret called, appropriately enough, Chicks with Dicks.

People in Thailand really don't make a lot of money. Being a ladyboy was a way for them to make money. Many hoped to meet a westerner or man from another country who would take care of them. Some visitors took care of them during the trip to Thailand, and some even took one home with them, which often meant taking care of the ladyboy's family as well.

Thailand is beautiful and gorgeous if you go at the right time of the year. I went in February and again in March. March was much hotter than February, so the best time to visit is probably between November and February. After that, it's a hot, sweaty sauna, worse than Florida in August, and it rains a lot during the summer. But it's worth seeing, especially if you like beaches, warm weather, and crystal blue waters.

You can also have just about any article of clothing that you like made or copied. I had boots made. The cobbler traced around my foot and told me to come back in three days, and the boots would be waiting for me. Because I was still doing the TV show and was very much into motorcycle wear, I also had leather jackets made and just about anything else I desired. All the goods were very inexpensive.

When it came to food, it was all fresh. You could walk down the street, pick out your lobster or the fish that you wanted, and they would take it to the back of the restaurant, cook it for you, and have it ready in a short amount of time.

In the morning, once I left the hotel for the beach, I pretty much didn't return until evening. After all, it was Thailand. It was casual, and no one cared if you ate dinner in your beach attire. But I have to say it was quite amusing watching the diners stare Stathis down as he walked into the restaurants in his Speedo. *Yes, I did say Speedo.* He was Greek and thought he was Adonis. I cringed every time, telling him, "Please put on a pair of shorts or at least a T-shirt." But he didn't care because everything is so laid-back and casual in Thailand. Plus, he was proud of that body!

We rode an elephant through the forest and jet skied all day. We sat in the water, drinking out of coconuts and pineapples, and checked out the local biker bar where you could rent a Harley-Davidson and go on a tour to the other side of the island. That, however, I declined, considering they drive on the opposite side of the road.

There were a lot of scooters and small motorcycles in Thailand. Sometimes you would see an entire family squeeze onto a single moped carrying a newborn baby, or you might see a man with a little handmade side platform where his goat or chicken stood as he drove down the road. In Phuket, such vehicles were the primary means of transportation.

I wouldn't be able to talk about Thailand without mentioning the December 26, 2004, tsunami and all the devastation left in its path, not only for the Thai people but also foreigners who were on Christmas holiday during that time.

One day as we were riding mopeds to one of the beaches, I asked Stathis, "Why is it that every time we ride past this area, I have a feeling of spirits and I get the chills?"

He said, "There used to be a hotel that stood here—a big hotel, and it was wiped out during the tsunami, and many people were killed."

Then it made sense to me that I had such a sad feeling passing by that area of the road.

I was in Thailand two years after the tsunami, and the locals told me stories. They said on that day, the beach was larger because the tide was many yards out from where it normally is. Most of the people who got up early in the morning were exercising by the water or taking their children to look for shells and play in the sand. It was the partiers who slept late.

And then there were locals who knew something was wrong that morning. The birds were quiet; in fact, all of the animals were quiet. There was something strange lingering, they told me. Some of the locals who recognized exactly what it was went far up into the mountains to get away from the beach, because they knew what was about to come.

At my hotel, I heard stories of how, right before the first wave hit, all the dishes and the silverware in the dining room started clanging and jingling. The wave was so forceful that it came into the hotel lobby, bringing with it automobiles, jet skis, motorcycles, and anything else in the street. People ran to the rooftop—others were running from the beach and climbing trees as the waves came crashing in.

But with a tsunami, it's not just the incoming waves that do damage. The wave goes back to sea, sucking everything out with it, and then it comes back again with even more force, knocking down electric lines, hotels, homes, trees, people—anything in its path. I remember seeing videos of the tsunami. Vendors were selling CDs on the street as well as magazines that showed devastating photographs. I couldn't even imagine what it must have been like for anyone who lived through that.

Stathis was actually there that year. Lucky for him, he stayed a few blocks back from the beach and was not by the shore that morning because he'd partied late and slept in. He did tell me stories of helping people in some of the markets who were dazed and confused.

And I will never forget the cover of one of the magazines—it might have been *Time*—which showed a Swedish family running away from the wave. You could see it behind them, coming after them with fury. Thankfully, they all survived.

We went on a small speedboat from Phuket to the Phi Phi (pronounced "pee pee") Islands, about an hour and a half away. In the distance, I could see beautiful mountains in the middle of the sea. It turned out to be an area in Thailand where Leonardo DiCaprio filmed his movie *The Beach*. I remember watching that movie back in early 2000 and thinking how beautiful this place was.

We stopped and swam a bit and then continued on to another area of the island. It was magnificent. Even with the destruction from the tsunami and missing hotels, the island was still a gorgeous treasure.

I have been there twice, both times for three weeks, and the words that describe Thailand are: *simply amazing!*

Run for the Roses! The Kentucky Derby, 2016.

If I could name one sporting event that seems to be on a lot of those "bucket lists," it would be The Kentucky Derby. Since 1875, there has been a Derby every year held on the first Saturday in May at Churchill Downs in Louisville, Kentucky—the ultimate party!

It's so exciting and thrilling to watch the race, which I attended in 2016. But the Kentucky Derby isn't just about the actual race on that day. There are all sorts of equally important events and parties during the weekend leading up to it.

The Longines Kentucky Oaks is a very important race for three-year-old fillies held the day before the actual Kentucky Derby. Because the race honors survivors of breast and ovarian cancer, in addition to raising money for those causes, the color of choice for both women and men on that day is pink.

The fashion at the Derby itself is a sight to behold, from suits and dresses to shoes. Of course, the most important part of one's wardrobe at the Kentucky Derby is *the hat*. I have seen all sorts of hats, which even have their own contest, including the homemade one a gentleman wore with a horse that ran around in a circle like it was racing. I have seen petite women wear hats that were literally bigger than they were.

Both men and women get in on the fashion traditions of the Kentucky Derby, and the more over the top, the better. Anything goes on Derby Day, from feathers to flowers to polka dots and more. It's like watching a parade, and a very lovely one at that!

There's so much color everywhere. You do not want to wear a little black dress to the Derby—no, no, no, nothing so boring! You must wear beautiful colors, whether florals, rainbows, plaids, or bold solids. I have seen men in flamingo suits and suits that appeared doused with multicolored paint. Then there are the men wearing flowered suits, jackets, and pants that perfectly match. It's so much fun to see. I give kudos to the men who go out on a limb and wear such colorful and wacky ensembles. And who doesn't love a bow tie on Derby Day?

I sat and watched the nonstop parade of wild fashion for two days. Some people were attending for the first time, but for many, it's a long-standing tradition. They look forward to the event every year. I can only imagine the time they take planning what they will wear from one year to the next.

Then there are the seats, from the outdoor seating in the stands around the track to different levels of indoor areas, each one costing more than the next. I was lucky enough to go first class all the way. I went with a friend who had loads of money to burn, and I had an in for some of the best seating in an area where the best party happened. *Lucky me!*

I was in the area where I could sit and people-watch, so much so it almost made me forget about the actual race, but I didn't care. I was more interested in watching all of the beautiful colored hats while sipping way too many (and way too strong) mint juleps—the official drink of the Kentucky Derby. But you have to be careful because they really pack a punch and a hangover!

Of course, another facet of the Derby is the betting. You wouldn't believe how much people lay down on Derby Day. Money was flying left and right.

As the lines for the betting windows grew longer, my friend handed me a stack of hundreds. He said in his thick accent, "Go make a bet for me to win on horse number so-and-so."

So I stood in the line with my stack, watching and listening to people talking about who they'd be betting on. I turned around at one point, and standing behind me was the actor Bill Paxton. I remember him mostly from the movie *Titanic*. We struck up a conversation and took a photo together. He seemed like a very kind person. Sadly, just a few months later, he passed away.

The lines for the betting windows were thick with people—rows and rows. People waiting to place bets struck up conversations with each other. In my line, a few guys in their mid-thirties seemed very excited to be there. They looked at the money I was holding and started telling each other, "Hey, we gotta bet on the horse she's picking. She's going to bet all that money—it's got to be a win!"

I thought to myself, *Oh, no, please don't.* My friend never had any good picks on horses; he'd pick a number and plunk down a shitload of money, only to lose almost every time. I would try to tell him, "Pick this one," or "Bet to win and win/place or win/place/show," but he never listened.

So I walked up to the window, handed the teller the stack, gave her the number, and got the ticket. Then I handed her one hundred bucks from my own money and picked Nyquist to win. And guess what happened? *Nyquist won!* My friend lost all his dough once again! But hey, as they say, it's only chips, right?

Yes, the Kentucky Derby was quite an experience!

In 2020 due to the pandemic, The Kentucky Derby was moved from May to September. The Derby ran without spectators. How sad and eerily quiet it must have been on that day at Churchill Downs.

ITALY, ROUND TWO: ROME, FLORENCE, VENICE

I finally went back to Italy in 2016. I'm not really sure what took me so long, but this time I went with a very wealthy friend from another country, the same friend with whom I attended the Kentucky Derby. I nicknamed him "My Money" because he was always worried about his money and how much was left in his bank account. He referred to his account as "my money," so I decided it was a great nickname for him as well.

I don't know why, but I seem to always attract the eccentric types, and I kind of like it. "My Money" was a very kind, sweet gentleman with a lovely accent. He was funny and interesting, and very discreet with his wealth. He wasn't the least bit showy but rather simple in a lot of ways, and I liked him for that. He wore nothing flashy and walked around in shorts and T-shirts with flip-flops that looked like slippers most of the time. He didn't care.

On one occasion when he knocked on my door in the morning to go out to breakfast, I had to remind him he was wearing the same T-shirt he'd worn the night before, and I could see stains on the front. He simply smiled and said, "Oh well, I like it—let's go." I just shook my head as people looked at him sometimes as if he had nothing, but I would smile when he would put down his credit card for a huge purchase. It was kind of like, *here, take that.*

"My Money" was quirky, odd, and sometimes very tight with a buck. He would rather park his Aston Martin in a dark alley at night than pay twenty dollars to keep it in the valet lot. And he really did obsess about his money. He checked his bank account balance so much during the day to make sure all his money was still there that I'm surprised he didn't wear out the letters on the keyboard of his laptop.

Sadly, "My Money" had a big drinking problem, but I didn't know just how big until we traveled together. There were times when he would stay in his room for twenty-four hours straight, not emerging until sometime the next afternoon when he was hungry. Then he would eat and go back to his room again. All the while I was at the beach, shopping, sightseeing, and exploring the cities.

To top it off, he was like Mr. Magoo when it came to keeping hold of his personal items. He was always losing something. He lost a credit card in an ATM machine and managed to leave a pair of Prada shoes in every Italian hotel room he occupied. He would literally leave things every place he went. Then there was his iPhone; to this day, I still don't know what happened to that one. I think he must have left it on an airplane seat.

It was all I could do to make sure he didn't lose his passport.

"My Money" would leave casinos with thousands of dollars of casino chips in a coat pocket. I once told him after we walked down three flights of stairs in a Venice casino that if I had to walk back up to cash all the chips he forgot about, *I was keeping the money.*

He said, "Okay, no problem." He was three sheets to the wind—he didn't care. So I asked the security to keep an eye on him until I made the trek back upstairs to cash in.

The next day he asked me, "Did I win or did I lose?" I laughed and said, "You lost—I won," referring to his chips. He said, "At least you're honest."

And then there was Florence. I don't think he even saw Florence because he stayed in his room the entire time. I explored the city on my own, and what a lovely city it was.

One morning, he knocked on my door and said he needed to go to the hospital. So I got him an ambulance, and off we went to the hospital in Florence. The doctor said essentially, "I can't do anything for him; he just drinks too much." *No shit, I told him the same thing.* They stuck some intravenous fluid in his arm, kept him for a few hours, and we left. You know the first thing he said when we left the hospital? "I need a vodka!"

When we were in Venice, we missed our train to Rome. I was so mad at him. Upon arriving back at the Venice hotel from which we had just checked out, the man at the front desk called me over and said, "Excuse me madam, the gentleman left his credit card in his room." I said, "It's a good thing we came back." As I was picking up his credit card, the man from the water taxi came looking for me and said, "Excuse me, but the gentleman left his iPhone on the water taxi." I said, "Of course he did, thank you."

Do you know how much the tips cost me during all these trips I made with him? *A lot.* Every time I turned around, a concierge or bellman was bringing me back something my friend had lost, and I felt obligated to tip them. That's why I kept the casino chips.

Good thing I managed to snap some photos of us on our European trips. About six months later when I heard from him again and we were having dinner, I showed him some of those pictures.

"Oh," he said, "we went to Italy?"

All I could do was smile.

RICHHHHH!

As I mentioned, I'm a magnet for eccentric people. And this next guy is one hell of an eccentric world traveler.

I can't remember exactly where, how, or when I met Don, but it was in the early days when I moved to Los Angeles. He was extremely funny and very entertaining—a talker, a mover, and a shaker, so to speak. He knew how to run his plate.

Don had a knack for befriending and traveling with anyone who was rich, and I'm talking mega rich. Even after thirty-three years, the first word out of his mouth whenever he sees or calls me is always the same: he yells out, "Rrrrriiiiiiiccccccchhhhhhhh-hhh!!!!... filthy...stinking...RICH!"

Don was the guy who introduced me to my Dutchman.

With my eccentric friend Don in Mexico.

He was living in Holland at the time, so when The Dutchman had business dealings, Don kept me entertained. On my first trip to Paris, he showed me all over the city and introduced me to some of his friends. When I went to London for the first time, it was Don who took me on a tour of the city, making sure I didn't miss anything and again introducing me to more friends.

He was a photographer, but not your typical photographer. To call him a paparazzo would be insulting. He never referred to himself as part of the paparazzi because he was more than that—he was someone who formed relationships with most of his celebrity clientele.

Don photographed celebrities, presidents, dignitaries, mayors, senators, diplomats, astronauts, princesses, princes, and kings. In one way or another, everyone he photographed was a person of importance.

Don traveled with The Dutchman on his private plane, lived in a hotel in Amsterdam provided by The Dutchman, and partied with The Dutchman and everyone else he met. And Don was really good at partying.

We'd travel together to the Cannes Film Festival every year, and if we needed tickets to a party or to the screening at the Palais, Don was the man. He knew everyone, everywhere in the world, and still does to this day.

All it took was one phone call and we had VIP passes to everything. And if for some reason he couldn't actually get the VIP passes, he figured out a way in. Like the year when he didn't have enough passes to get into the Palais screening: he gave us all the passes, but in order to get himself in, he just held his camera up in front of his face and started photographing us, walking backward right into the building.

I remember one year when The Dutchman arrived at the Nice airport, Don phoned a friend who was high up in the security world and had The Dutchman escorted from Nice into Cannes, a forty-five-minute ride, with flashing lights and sirens raging on the car all the while to get through the festival traffic. Don was nuts but fun nuts!

He was the kind of person who would wave to a celebrity and say, "Hey, Michael Jackson" or "Hey, Elizabeth Taylor" or President So-and-So or whoever the celebrity might be. "How are you doing?" he would ask. "We met at such-and-such a place, remember? Can I take a picture with my friend...?" They all knew him and always obliged.

Most of my pictures with celebrities from the film festival years were possible because of Don. He once walked up to Jon Voight and said, "Michele, stand next to Jon. Let's take a photo."

Another time, he said, "Stand next to Bo" (as in Bo Derek). We always got the shot. Most of the time, he would just call the celebrity by their first name, and none of them ever stopped him.

I watched Don walk onto private yachts of people he hardly knew and say, "Hey, Mr. So-and-So, remember me?" The next thing you know, he was sipping champagne and eating caviar on someone's yacht, having dinner and making plans to sail off into the sunset to some exotic location with the owner!

It was as if no one ever said no to Don. He was just so damn entertaining. I would laugh until my face hurt and my sides split.

Don still has a way of working his magic on people. He is constantly on private jets and private yachts, dining at the finest restaurants around the world, smoking the best cigars, drinking the most expensive wines, and taking the most amazing photographs of people some photographers only dream of shooting. If you didn't actually know him and heard him telling all his stories, you'd think this guy is full of shit. But he's not—he lived it.

His collection of photographs must be worth a fortune, and the funny thing is he doesn't just photograph these people—in most cases, he actually befriends them.

We've lost touch over the years, but from time to time, I will check in with him to find out where in the world he is.

The last time I talked to him, he said he was with Prince So-and-So at the palace in Abu Dhabi but would be leaving the following week on his private plane to France. He then proceeded to give a long list of countries and cities on his itinerary, which ended with Los Angeles. He hasn't changed, and it's hard to keep up with him.

Don must be well into his seventies by now, but he's lived an amazing life and his saga continues even after all these years. *Now that's a life well lived!*

SOME PEOPLE

Have you ever noticed how some people just cannot enjoy themselves on a holiday? I hate to say it, but most of those people are my fellow Americans.

Listen, you should get out and see the world, but you should enjoy it at the same time! Over and over again I have said life is meant to be lived...live your life...go...put your ass on the plane, or a bus, or a train, or in your car, and go see something.

And if you're one of those people who says, "I have no desire to see the old country," or "I'm happy right here," *well, travel doesn't mean you need to leave the country!* Go anywhere! Broaden your horizons. You never know what you might get out of it or how much time you have left on Earth.

Just remember one thing if you travel abroad: you are venturing into a new culture, a new way of life, and a different language.

You should remember that not everyone will speak English, nor should they be expected to. In fact, it wouldn't hurt if you looked up a few words of the language of the country you're visiting. Learn some basics like please, thank you, good evening, and good morning in advance. If you try just a little bit, your efforts will be appreciated.

I have watched some people complaining, even fighting, with foreigners because they do not speak English. *Hello, you are in their country!*

Yes, I understand a language barrier can be frustrating, but there's always a way to figure it out and make a trip pleasurable for everyone.

And then there's the matter of food. Go on, just try it and enjoy it, because I have to tell you, champagne tastes a whole lot better in another country than it does at home.

There's nothing more enjoyable to me than sitting in the

square of a foreign country at a beautiful little café, people-watching and drinking a lovely glass of wine, champagne, beer, or even plain water! It just tastes so much better.

Don't be that person out on a mission to find a McDonald's. You have McDonald's every day of the week at home. *You are in a new country, a new place, on a new adventure, so dig in*—you just might surprise yourself. Even if you are looking to eat cheap on a budget, grab a sandwich from one of the local shops. Trust me: you'll probably enjoy it.

And please put aside anything you have ever heard in advance about the people of the country you are traveling to.

For example, the French are NOT assholes. Again, if you manage to pick up a few basic words from Google (I'm not talking about going out and paying for a whole course with Rosetta Stone), it will go a long way.

And *be polite.* Did you ever think that the French people who you thought were rather rude might just be a bit intimidated because they feel their English isn't up to par? It doesn't mean they are assholes.

When it comes to the Dutch, oh please, don't even get me started on that one. How often have you heard the term "Dutch treat"? It's not true. I have never once experienced a cheap Dutchman in all my years of spending time in Holland. The Dutch people I knew were all kind, generous, and welcoming, and I was never once asked to split the bill.

Not all Persians and Iranians are carpet dealers, and not all Columbians are drug or arms dealers.

Now, in some countries, what you hear could be true. Take for example the Greeks: yes, most of the ones I've met are Greek gods.

And what about the Italians? Those flirty, beautiful men who grab you on the street! Well, yes, it's true—I have been grabbed.

As far as the English being uptight or stuffy, I have known some pretty funny Englishmen—hysterically funny, actually. I would throw back a pint with them any day. I think they have a wonderful sense of humor!

I could go on and on about the myths of other countries, but I'll leave it at that.

Please open your mind, open your heart, and keep a kind smile when you travel. It will make the most out of your experience.

THE SCENT OF TRAVEL

For me, travel has a scent. Every city has something that reminds me of where I am or where I was.

I could smell roasted chestnuts anywhere in the world, but it always reminds me of New York City in the fall. The smell of charcoal on a grill reminds me of a park in Pennsylvania I went to as a kid.

And then there is perfume; I am a big lover of perfumes, pretty much all of them. Sometimes if I'm shopping, I will just keep testing and spraying until I walk out of the shop smelling like one big walking whorehouse, and I don't care.

I became that way from all the time I spent in the South of France. I would walk by a shop and get a whiff of...something. At first, I couldn't quite figure out what it was, but after smelling the same scent at a few of the shops, I realized it was a mix of patchouli and amber—two scents that I have come to find most people do not like! I, on the other hand, love them both, especially amber.

There have been a lot of things written about patchouli. Some say it has an earthy smell and describe it as the unwashed cousin of lavender. There is a theory that it's an aphrodisiac and was used by the Egyptians for mummification, and for years I've heard "it's a hippie scent" because it was used to hide the smell of marijuana. ***Then I guess I'm a bit of a hippie!***

I would go to Grasse, a city up in the hills about twenty-five minutes from Cannes, and walk through the perfume factories. I watched as the person behind the glass tested and sniffed the fragrances. He was called a "nose." I found it all very interesting.

Often I would buy loads of perfumes and send them back to the States. Call it eccentric, but whenever I had a party or a get-together in my home, I would pour the perfumes in the toilets and sometimes even add rose petals. ***Hey, whatever makes you feel good.***

So of course the combination of amber and patchouli reminds me of Cannes or Saint-Tropez, especially the little turquoise shop on the corner of the Rue d'Antibes where you don't even have to walk inside to get a whiff.

Whenever I'm in France, I go directly to those shops where I know that scent will be.

I often spritz my home with the same scents just to remind me of France in the summertime.

Certain scents remind me of being in a city in Europe and elsewhere, but sometimes it isn't only a city—it could even be a certain month. The fragrance Samsara still reminds me of Amsterdam in December, while Boucheron reminds me of Amsterdam any other time of the year.

And then there is London, where I used to ***pay a pound to pee***, as I called it, in the Harrods restroom. It was worth the pound just to get a spritz of the perfume in the bathrooms! It was like perfume du jour!

There was also a fragrance from Egypt that I love. I cannot for the life of me find out what the name is—even though I have the empty bottle. Nothing is written on it anymore. I bought it thirty years ago in what Harrods called the Salon de Parfum.

It's a beautiful little turquoise bottle with a super sweet smell, almost too sweet, but it reminds me of London, and Harrods in particular.

The scent of Issey Miyake reminds me of Greece—mainly because one of my Greek gods loved it.

Louis Vuitton has a fragrance called Attrape-Rêves, which reminds me of Santiago, Chile.

Whenever I wear Chanel, I am reminded of my very entertaining friend Bill, who for many years worked the Chanel counter and always sent me bags of Chanel goodies.

I could go on and on about different scents that remind me of a city or a time. Most of the fragrances are from a time long ago, and I don't wear them anymore—but if I want to remember a certain time in my life, I know it's just a scent away!

EATING AROUND THE WORLD

Eating freeze-dried frogs in Thailand, 2005.

Champagne always tastes better in France, even in a wineglass!

And then there's the food!

There were two things I would constantly eat in the South of France: the salad niçoise (no anchovies) and the goat cheese salad. Like I said, champagne just tastes better in France. Actually food and everything else just tastes better in France. I'm normally not a big dessert person, but whenever I'm in France,

I go for the chocolate mousse. In fact, I'm not even a big chocolate person, but there's something about that chocolate mousse in France that is so rich and so tasty that I can't resist.

When I'm in LA, I go to the little French place at the Farmers Market, and I always eat the salad niçoise because it reminds me of the South of France.

A few years ago, I stayed at the Hôtel Byblos in Saint-Tropez and ordered a $200 crab salad. I swear to you it was the best damn salad I ever ate in my life. I came home and tried to re-create it, but I could never get it to taste the same. I told my girlfriend in LA about it. Two weeks later, she went to the Byblos with her son, and they both ordered that same crab salad. Ha! I think they were curious after I told them how good (and expensive) it was.

Galatia, Spain, where I walked the Camino de Santiago, is known for little almond cakes with the Cross of Saint James stenciled in powdered sugar on top. The cross is a common symbol along the Camino and in most of the shops. I loved those little cakes not so much for the taste but just because they were so pretty, and I love the Camino cross. You can find them everywhere in that region, where they are better known as Spanish almond cakes.

Ooooh, Amsterdam! It was nice sometimes just to have a very simple meal of bread and cheese, or as they call it, *klein broodje*. We'd walk into little shops that were quite busy during the lunch hour, where the Dutch would go for a quick, inexpensive bite. They were more like a diner or deli—very simple. Holland isn't really known for a specific food, but the cheese is fantastic.

And pizza in Italy—*just plain old margherita pizza, cheese with thin crust, the way little cafés in Italy make it in the pizza ovens.* But the best part is watching the Italians eat pizza, which you can also see in the Italian places in the South of France. I call it the art of eating pizza!

First of all, they take a big, round, unsliced pizza. Using a fork and a knife, they start eating it—sometimes from the middle. I have seen plates go back to the kitchen that have the entire middle eaten with just a perfect ring of crust left around the edge. I love watching people eat their pizza in Italy and France. They savor every delicious bite of it, and their way is much nicer than someone folding over a slice and stuffing it in their mouth!

PUSHED BY A GHOST

In 2018, my friend Steve said I should stay in his apartment while I was back in Los Angeles. He had a place in the Hollywood Tower Apartments in east LA on Franklin Ave.

You might have heard the Tower of Terror at Disney was named after that apartment complex—so the story goes. Legend has it that in 1939, when the Hollywood Tower was actually a hotel, the regular elevators were out of order, so five people took the service elevator from the top floor. A storm was raging, lightning struck, and the car fell to the ground, killing everyone inside. After that, the hotel closed and later became apartments.

The deadly incident happened on Halloween night, and it's said the spirits still inhabit the property.

Well, it just so happened I was going to stay in the Hollywood Tower Apartments the week of Halloween...*go figure.*

As I drove up to the place, I remembered exactly what it was and where it was, and I thought to myself, *Oh shit, not THAT building—why did I agree to stay here?*

The building's entrance looks like the opening scene from

a horror film. You immediately get the sense that something's not right. From the exterior architecture to the parking garage, there's a heavy feeling of doom.

I thought about turning around and going to a hotel, but I didn't want to disappoint my friend or make him feel bad, thinking that his place wasn't good enough for me to stay in. But honestly, *what was I thinking?*

My friend's girlfriend had told me how they wanted to interview him for one of the ghost TV shows, but he didn't want anything to do with it. I don't know if he didn't want to talk about the ghosts or it freaked him out too much. Whatever the reason, he declined to do the interview. Well, let me tell you, I could have done that interview for him.

I walked into the lobby and looked around at the 1930s decor. My feelings were mixed. I wasn't sure what to think, not knowing what was behind the dusty, floor-length, velvet curtains that hung at the bottom of that dark staircase I'd have to pass by every day for a week.

There was a man at the front desk, one of the few people I actually saw the entire time I was there.

Strange.

He offered to take my bags up to the apartment because the elevator wasn't working. It turned out the elevator didn't work that entire Halloween week. I'm not sure why. I don't know whether it was a coincidence or if the elevators were taken out of service on the anniversary of the deadly accident.

I entered the apartment and looked around. It was one of those old, very spacious, beautiful places with wood floors, high ceilings, and arched windows like the original apartments around old Hollywood.

But this one had something extra special that I could have done without. I wasn't thinking too much about the spirits, although I did notice that my friend kept a baseball bat by the front door. I don't know if that was for the ghosts or for people trying to break in; after all, it was the east side of Hollywood.

My first night there, I was lying in bed around eleven o'clock at night, just dozing off, when I felt someone tickling my feet. Bizarre, I know! I started laughing and thought to myself, *Am I dreaming? Come on, this can't really be happening!* Crazy, right?

Just as I was thinking to myself that there was no way this could be true, a powerful force pushed me sideways! I had been lying with my feet pointing south, but I was pushed so hard that now my feet were pointing west. It was as if someone took their fist and pushed my ass with all their might, turning me like the hand on a clock. I jumped out of bed, turned every single light on in the apartment, and stayed up for the rest of the night. Had it been ten years earlier, I know I would've packed my stuff and left for a hotel, but this event intrigued me. It was the first time I'd ever had physical contact with a spirit.

The next day, I went to the local health food store and purchased the biggest bundle of sage I could find. Then I went to the Farmers Market and purchased a palo santo. I burned both of them in every inch and corner of that apartment. I told the spirit, "Whoever you are, you have to leave." I opened the windows and the door, and I said, "Get out. You're not welcome here." I was staying until Tuesday, so I told the spirit, "You can come back on Wednesday." I wanted to make sure there were no delays to my flight.

I called my friend right after it happened, and he and his girlfriend were dying laughing. They said they had heard about the presence but had never had contact with it or felt it. My friend told me it was supposedly a woman.

After reading the story of the Tower, which I'd refused to read before I stayed there, I'm thinking perhaps the presence who came to visit me was the child actress who died that night in the elevator—tickling my feet like a child would do.

I must say after I burned all the sage and palo santo in the apartment, I never felt the presence of a spirit again. The rest of the Tower was a little different. During the week when I would come back from spending time out with my friends, I'd race up the steps from the dark, dingy, cold parking garage, through the art deco lobby, and then up another huge flight of stairs and past the long dusty velvet curtains. To this day, I do not know what was behind those curtains. Then I would run down the hallway, especially on Halloween night, like something out of a horror movie. I ran so fast that I swear I felt my hair blowing straight back in the wind. The door to my friend's apartment was the last door on the left. *Ha...just like a horror film.*

Recently when I told my friend I was going to LA, he said, "Will you be staying in the apartment?" I just shook my head and said, "No, thank you!"

PEOPLE-WATCHING

I have often thought that people-watching should be a sport.

Think about it: you pay money to go to sporting events, some of which are over very quickly, like the Mike Tyson fight I once went to. But you get to watch people for free, and it's often very entertaining.

Bigger cities like LA are usually the most enjoyable places to watch people.

Once, early in the morning, I watched as a young man walked out of his apartment in the Melrose Place area of Los Angeles with a pig on a leash. Now, I'm not talking about one of those cute little potbellied pigs here. I'm talking about an actual farm animal pig. *Huge.*

They walked casually down the street as if he were walking a dog, and nobody seemed to notice or care. Nor did anyone care when the girl dressed in the little green fairy outfit with wings walked the streets of Hollywood early in the mornings. Nothing seems to faze the City of Angels, and that's the best part of LA—*anything goes!*

Then there is the "ladies who lunch" kind of people-watching in places like Beverly Hills and Miami—*so much fun.* I love everything from checking out all of the sexy women with perfect bodies in tiny outfits in Miami at a popular lunch hangout, to the Birkin bags and designer clothing of women lunching in Beverly Hills. Not to mention the plastic surgery— *oh, the plastic surgery!*

I try to guess who had what done, lips being a dead giveaway in both places. I once ran into a woman I had not seen for many years. She was a nurse but now does all sorts of injections, from lips to facial to Botox and more. I hardly recognized her through all the fillers she had done to herself, but the first words out of her mouth were, "Oh, so nice to see you! Wow, I'm surprised you haven't had any kind of filler or injections! You really need it! You should come see me." I said, "Okay, thank you." What else could I say? Apparently I hadn't had enough Botox to please her. *Sooooo LA!*

The trick to people-watching is hiding behind a great pair of sunnies or maybe taking a half look out of the corner of your eye, pretending not to be watching, depending on the city you're in. One would never really want to be caught gazing!

I especially love people-watching in other parts of the world. But sometimes what we think about a person is not always the truth. I watched a young girl in Thailand who walked up and down the beach all day long in the hot sun, selling her goods. She finally arrived at my chair, and I asked her how old she was.

She was barely twelve, and she said she had to quit school to help her mom, who was sick.

In Thailand, we never really knew if the stories we heard were the truth or fictions created to make the money needed for the day. In this case, I gave the young girl her money and told her to take a break. Whether her story was real or not didn't matter—she told a good one, and perhaps she really needed the money.

I have watched people hustle to make money around the world: from the drivers outside airports in foreign cities (who, by the way, are not really proper taxi drivers and you should proceed with caution), to the guys who flag you down and direct you into their shops to sell you a souvenir, to the men in Rome selling tickets to get you to the front of the line at the Vatican, and more.

It's part of what makes people-watching so interesting.

Some of my best people-watching took place in Santiago, Spain, and also turned out to be a good learning experience. One day before I started walking the Camino, I sat with my girlfriend in a café, eating, drinking wine, and watching all the Camino pilgrims end their journey—stumbling into Santiago to the Cathedral of Saint James. As we watched these people with walking sticks hobbling barefoot, with bandaged feet, or in socks, some being held up by a friend because their feet were so blistered, we looked at each other and said, "Oh my, will this be us in a week?" I think it was at that point I went out and purchased more Compeed (blister patches) to make sure I had enough for the walk.

And then there are the very over-the-top romantic couples I have seen in numerous places around the world, totally going at it in public. So much PDA! You want to say, "Hey, go get a room," but you can't. They are enjoying the moment, so good for them.

Ahhh, yes, people-watching—what great entertainment!

THE CAMINO DE SANTIAGO

Along the Camino French Way, 2019.

If you've seen the movie *The Way* with Martin Sheen, then you've heard about the Camino de Santiago in Spain. That film was my introduction to the Camino and my inspiration. It made me very curious, and I wanted to learn more.

The Camino, which is also known as the Way of Saint James,

is a network of ancient pilgrimage routes, all of which lead to Santiago de Compostela, Spain. The Camino has been a pilgrimage route for over 1,000 years. It is said to have been started when early Christians undertook the trek across the country from wherever they lived to the Santiago de Compostela Cathedral, or Cathedral of Saint James, where the body of Saint James is believed to be buried.

One route, which many consider to be the "official" route, is the Camino Francés, a 500-mile pilgrimage across northern Spain, with all of its history. People say spiritual things happen to you on the Camino. Pilgrims walk it for many reasons, and some are dying of cancer or have lost their limbs and are pushed along the Camino in wheelchairs. People of all ages and all walks of life come to the Camino for personal and spiritual reasons.

After watching *The Way*, I thought about walking the Camino a lot over the years but wasn't sure it was possible for me to do. I wanted to make the trek or at least part of it, as there are several shorter stretches of the Camino that you can walk rather than tackling the full 500 miles all at once. I thought you had to stay in the wilderness in a tent and knew that just wouldn't be feasible for me, a woman traveling alone. It was only in the past couple of years that I started hearing more about the Camino and decided to look into it further.

I'm not sure if all of a sudden it was becoming a trendy thing to do, but I began meeting more people who told me they'd walked it, some in groups and some on their own. So I found an agency in Ireland and contacted them to get the details. They told me they would organize everything for me; all I had to do was send the money. They sent me an itinerary that consisted of a total of eight days, six of which would involve walking, for a total of eighty-three miles. They arranged the hotel rooms, the guide, the meals—everything! And I wouldn't have to carry a heavy backpack, only a day pack. They would take my luggage via car from hotel to hotel so that when I arrived, everything was already there.

It sounded like a plan to me! I was looking for something different and more meaningful and exciting to do during the summer than going back to the South of France and lying on the beach. The truth is, I was bored shitless sitting on the beach—*same old, same old.* This voice in me was saying, *I'm not going to sit around for another summer. I'm not doing this.* And no, I did not train for the Camino at all. I simply just said, *I'm going to do this—I'm going to walk at my own pace with a lot of Compeed,* and off I went.

At the very last minute, my friend Lori from LA decided to come, too. We started in reverse because we arrived in Santiago. Lori and I walked around Santiago and saw people finishing the Camino, limping along barefoot, their feet a complete mess, barely able to walk! We were thinking, *OMG, that's gonna be us!* We saw one guy with a big stick and bare feet. He was limping and could hardly get through the streets. I wondered, *Am I really gonna be able to do this?*

Walking the Camino de Santiago was definitely one of the greatest experiences of my life because it was something I never thought I'd be able to do. I never believed I'd be able to walk eighty-three miles in six days without being an avid walker or athlete. I had so many naysayers telling me I'd never make it. I'm glad I didn't listen to them.

After our arrival in Santiago, the tour company drove us to the starting point. We began our eighty-three-mile walk in Sarria, which was about a two-hour drive from Santiago but much longer on foot. In Sarria, our guide gave us our Camino passports, which we'd get stamped when we stopped at bars, cafés, restaurants, and churches along the way. When you complete the walk, your passport is filled with stamps from all these different locations, proof that you actually walked and didn't cheat by grabbing a taxi.

In the end, you take your Camino passport to an office where they issue your official certificate to show that you finished your walk.

When I got my certificate, I was so excited. I overcame the naysayers, which is one of the reasons I wanted to do it! Yes, I got a few blisters, but not as many as some of the other people. And yes, my legs were swollen, but I got up every day and did the same thing over and over again for six days. Perhaps the swollen legs and the blisters didn't bother me so much because about every two hours or so, I stopped at the pubs and restaurants along the way to have a lovely glass of wine or an icy cold beer with lemon. For me, those interludes were actually one of the best parts of walking the Camino! I met all sorts of people along the way, from places all over the world. Then, after twenty minutes or so, I got back up and moved on.

I saw people of all ages. I saw little kids three and four years old, some who walked and some being pushed in a stroller. I heard one French mother say, "I would rather be here with my son than have him sitting in front of the TV all summer." I saw elderly men and women well into their eighties and possibly even their nineties walking. Everyone walked at their own pace. There were people walking as if they were in a race, people walking slowly, and people with blisters on their feet struggling to make it to the end. Most of them did, and yes, I was one of those people. We walked an average of something more than thirteen miles a day.

My friend Lori wore tennies and didn't get a single blister. I wore hiking boots and wool socks, and I had a whole ritual every morning for my feet. It involved Leukotape on the bottom of my feet and took about twenty-five minutes. I ended up with one blister. Totally worth it.

We walked through farmlands and stopped at farmhouses where the fine people of Galicia opened their homes and served food to Camino pilgrims. The Galicians are very hospitable and set up tables where you can stop and eat and drink. These are incredibly generous men and women! I'm saddened to hear some of those places have disappeared now, as the whole area was hit hard by the pandemic. Hospitality for pilgrims was the livelihood of the region.

We walked on dirt roads, stone roads, paved roads, through the woods, up hills, down hills—we walked and walked and walked, and drank wine and beer and more wine! We walked through cemeteries and herds of goats, cows, and horses. If we'd been in the States, we wouldn't have looked twice at a cow or horse, but on the Camino, we were enthralled.

We stayed in different hotels along the way, but the one that stood out for me the most was a beautiful old farmhouse out in the country with only nine rooms. It was gorgeous and very old, and I somehow knew just by looking at the photo, even before I went on the trip, that it was haunted or had some sort of spirits.

It was a family-owned farmhouse, and upon arrival, the son who ran the hotel handed us each a key to our rooms. Lori mentioned to me that he looked at each of us and then looked down at the keys, as if deciding which number he would match with us. I hadn't noticed. I think I was too interested in the interior of this place, looking at the decor with all its ancient beauty.

Once in my room, I unpacked my suitcase and took out the palo santo that I'd brought with me. I had saved it especially for this day. I opened the shutter windows in my room and had a view of an old church with a graveyard.

Palo santo is used to clear out negative energy. So I had it with me because of the photos of the farmhouse I'd seen. I just had a feeling.

No sooner did I pull it out of the bag and lay it on the nightstand than I felt a presence in the room. I didn't even have time to light my palo santo! The presence beat me to the punch, and it was strong. I cannot explain it. I do not know where it came from. Maybe it was because I wanted some spiritual thing to happen on the Camino, or maybe it was because I had a feeling in advance something was going to be in this farmhouse.

I don't know if it was something that came out of or had to do with the picture of Jesus on the wall, but I can tell you this: it was not a bad presence, just some force of energy that came over me. I started crying, but it wasn't a bad thing. I sat there for what felt like ten minutes, and then just as quickly as it came, it left—and everything was normal again.

Of the few photos I took at the farmhouse the next morning when we were all in the breakfast room, two or three have an orb behind each person.

That beautiful farmhouse in the country did not scare me, and I know that one day I will go back again and ask for the room with Jesus on the wall.

There is so much to be said about the Camino de Santiago that it could be an entire book of its own. I walked the French way, which is the shortest way, because I figured I had to start somewhere. I needed to see if I could even make the trek without hopping in a taxi, and I did make it.

Walking into the city of Santiago, we saw other pilgrims limping in, some with a single walking stick, some with two walking sticks, some in bare feet because they could just no longer wear shoes from all the blisters. But they finished and made it to the Cathedral of Saint James, and so did I! I remember thinking, *Wow, I did this*, as we walked into Santiago.

I will be back again on the Camino in the future when I know the cathedral is no longer under construction. I missed the swinging of the Botafumeiro, a large incense burner that swings high from the cathedral ceiling. It was out of commission when I was there due to the construction. Making a trip back would be worth it just for that.

¡Buen Camino!

PART VI

Lockdown

So You Know…

IT TOOK A LOCKDOWN TO KEEP ME IN ONE PLACE, AND I actually didn't mind it. I needed the downtime. Oddly enough, in some ways I am a homebody—at least when I'm in town. When I travel, I like to go as far away as possible, but when I'm home, I like to enjoy my house, my peace, and my surroundings.

I had plenty of time to reflect. And, after going through thousands of photos and mementos, mostly for research for this book, I came to realize how much I've really done in my life.

I looked at photos of celebrities that I'd met and print advertisements I'd appeared in, as well as watching videos I found of myself in commercials or ads that I didn't even remember doing. I guess I was just so busy, and once I did one job, I would move on to the next one, never stopping to realize the importance of what I'd just done.

So I'm glad that the pandemic and lockdown slowed me down enough to reflect and actually see what I've accomplished. And it led me to truly value all the traveling I've done.

I think it's important to travel! It's a chance to get out and open up your mind to new possibilities and experiences. You never know what you might find or discover about yourself or who you might meet just going one town away. New adventures can be fun and interesting—getting away from your everyday routine can be energizing.

On my travels, I've always had my angels watching over me. I think everyone has angels watching over them, but not everyone believes in all of that, so perhaps they don't feel them. You have to believe. Some things happen in life that we can't explain, and for me, it's always about the angels—even if one dozed off and forgot to watch me on that day. ***Hey, shit happens, even with the angels...***

THE PANDEMIC

My pandemic project!

I had a lot of time to think during the lockdown. I spent time combing through my life like a movie, looking through old photo albums and remembering all that I have accomplished.

I started saying to myself, *I guess I've had a lot of experiences in my life.* Looking at some of the photos I have, especially those from the Cannes Film Festival, I realized I'd rubbed elbows with many celebrities and producers without realizing it—or maybe I just didn't care. My life was a whirlwind, and I was in my own world for many years.

For most of those years, my sister had told me, "You should keep a diary of all your travels." I would respond, "Diaries are dangerous." People told me numerous times that I should keep a journal or write a book—even people who hardly knew me but had heard some of my stories. I always laughed it off, until now.

Looking back made me think maybe my friends and family were right and I should write about all my experiences. I have seen things and done things that most people never get to do in a lifetime.

I spent the lockdown in South Florida.

While everyone else was freezing in the North or locked up in small apartments with no balconies, my ass was floating on a raft in the pool. Sorry, I feel like I need to apologize for having said I had a wonderful quarantine.

The world needed a lockdown. Look at what happened with our rivers, oceans, and air—pollution decreased, and the skies were clear. I look at it as a cleansing period for the Earth.

And yes, it was also a horrific time because we lost many people to this horrible virus. For that I am deeply saddened. I cannot imagine losing a loved one, without the ability to be with them in the hospital during their final moments. I don't believe anyone should ever have to be alone in the end.

That is one reason I am thankful my parents were already

long gone and didn't have to suffer through something like COVID-19.

I am deeply sorry for all the people, families, children, and even animals who had to suffer through this terrible and frightening pandemic. Hopefully the future for everyone will be much brighter.

I know I have had enough of a big break from life during the pandemic, and I'm ready to get back on the road again and in the skies.

Don't get me wrong: I actually loved the long overdue break from life's daily routine, and it did take a pandemic to actually slow me down, but I'm not one to stay in one place for any length of time. I'm like a fidgety kid who can't sit still.

Truth be told, five months into the pandemic, I couldn't take it any longer. So with many precautions—including double-masking, hand sanitizer, and Lysol for the plane—off I went to visit family in Pennsylvania.

Then I went back to LA, staying at a hotel without any service, and the only guest on my floor was me! It was an uneasy feeling at times, but I was so happy to be back on the West Coast and out of the house that I didn't care if there wasn't any service.

I left LA in the nick of time before everything got shut down for a second time and for a longer period.

But I still missed traveling abroad and hated to be told I couldn't. So in the middle of the pandemic, as I was sitting at home, I decided to create my own little retreat in my yard and installed a clawfoot bathtub in an area behind my house. It feels like a bohemian, *Gilligan's Island*, hidden-in-the-garden getaway, but it's so nice to sit outside soaking in a tub, especially in the early mornings while enjoying the sounds of nature. And it gave me another project to work on.

I have always been one of those people who is more comfortable living out of a suitcase than staying in one place for too long. People frequently asked me, "Do you ever get tired of being on the road?" And my answer was always no, never.

I thought at some point, especially by age sixty, I would want to relax and chill, but it hasn't happened yet. A friend said to me recently, "How do you have so much energy? You're like a five-year-old! You're always moving around doing something." I said I honestly don't know. I keep waiting for the day when I have to take an afternoon nap, and I hope that day never comes.

I overheard a conversation the other day in a store. It was between two ladies in their seventies who were talking about how tired they are and all the medicines that they were taking. And then the one said her husband always has to take a nap in the afternoon, when he used to be so active. All I could think of was, *Oh, no, is that going to be me one day?* I don't want that to be what I have to look forward to for my future. And I don't want to be the lady with the Monday through Sunday box of pills!

My age is sixty, but my mind at times is thirty; what can I say? Age is only a number, and although I wish I could somehow change mine to a much lower one, there isn't a damned thing I can do about it. So I just make the best of it and "think young"—keep moving!

WHERE TO NEXT?

Being locked up with nowhere to go and being told to stay in one place gave me such a strange feeling. When I did go out, the highways and streets were eerily empty. My neighborhood, however, was a different story. I have never seen so many people out walking and riding bicycles—people I had never met, seen ever before, or even known existed.

It seemed like such a bizarre time in the world. That our

hands had been tied and we had been cut off from travel and the rest of the world was so unthinkable—especially no overseas travel! It was something I never could have imagined happening in my life. Thinking back about lockdown still seems unreal to me, almost like a bad dream.

Lately I have been thinking about where my next destination will be. There are still many places I need to see. Morocco is definitely one of them, with its beautiful, brightly colored markets and amazing foods. I know there is a camel waiting for me somewhere in Morocco to escort me on a ride through the desert. I can imagine myself enjoying every aspect of it.

And for years I have seen the photos of those sexy little huts over the turquoise waters of the Indian Ocean in the Maldives. It looks like an amazing destination to sit, relax for a while, bathe in the sea, and bake in the warmth of the sun while sipping a lovely glass of champagne. But the Maldives would probably be boring without a companion, so I may need to think about who I could put up with on such a long trip. Or who could put up with me!

Recently, I heard about a place in Bali called the Firefly Eco Lodge. The rooms are big bamboo bird's nests. I may just need to go back to Bali and this time spend at least one night while I can still make the climb high into the trees.

The bird's nests are four-story huts built of bamboo woven into a nest, with beds nestled inside each one. You climb a steep ladder to reach your nest, depending on how high you want to go. The higher up, the better the view. Sleeping inside a nest sounds like a one-of-a-kind experience, and I'd love to say I was a bird for a night. Why not?

When it feels right, and I think the world is totally back in the swing of things, I will head out once again to some amazing place, one I haven't seen yet. Or maybe I will just toss a coin or close my eyes and point to something on the map. So be it—wherever my finger lands, is where I will go!

My list goes on and on, but as I have said before, I don't really make a bucket list. It's pretty much where I feel I want to go in that moment. I'll know it when I wake up one day and it's on my mind. So it's not like I can always plan a trip in advance. I get a feeling, and when I get something in my head, that's it.

In fact, I think the only personal trip I have ever planned more than two weeks in advance was walking the Camino, but that was mostly because I had to tell myself months in advance that I could do it. I had to mentally prepare more than physically prepare. And it worked. Thank God I only listened to myself and ignored the people who said I would never make it.

I am sometimes a creature of habit when it comes to travel. But I'm trying to get myself out of that mode. If I like a place and I get to know it well, I tend to return again and again. I enjoy going back to the cafés that I know, shopping at my favorite boutiques, and seeing friends I have met on previous travels. Sometimes I just miss something so much—like the smell of the South of France or that familiar face in a shop in Mykonos—that I want to return again. I suppose it's the familiarity of everything that I like. To know I can travel so far away and still see someone I know or a familiar place is comforting. I think most of it is because I am almost always a solo traveler. I feel more comfortable going to places where I know I can navigate my way around and feel good being there on my own.

I am, however, starting to get myself out of that mode. As I get older, I keep telling myself that I have to go to more new places. Some people would rather stay home and only dream about exotic destinations than travel solo. But if I did that, I would never see anything.

Why wait for someone to come along to travel with? Sometimes you just have to pick yourself up and go. After all, you never know who you will meet along the way. I have made friends during my travels in many countries. It keeps life fun and interesting. And we all need something to pick us up in our lives, especially after being in a severe lockdown for so many months.

So as far as where a plane will take me next—I'll just have to wait and see.

DYK?

In my life and travels, I've come across the ironic, the inappropriate, and the downright weird. Did you know...

In Hershey, Pennsylvania, the streetlights are Hershey's Kisses, some wrapped in silver foil and others chocolate, just like the candy.

In Etters, Pennsylvania, there is a convenience store called Rutter's where you can not only buy gas and food but also attend a wine tasting, paired with Skittles and other candies. (Hey, it's a convenience store in the country!) Yep, it's true. To top it off, they even have slot machines. Gas, gambling, wine tastings, and even frozen margaritas, all under one convenient convenience store roof! Who would have thought?

In the state of Pennsylvania, there are several towns with sexual names:

- Intercourse
- Blue Ball
- Bird in Hand
- Fertility

By the way, they're all located in Lancaster County, in Amish country. *I wonder what the Amish had in mind when they named these towns?*

In Lynchburg, Tennessee, they've been making Jack Daniels whiskey for more than 150 years. But this tiny town with a population of just over 6,000 is in a dry county. Excuse me? I rode a motorcycle there from Franklin, Tennessee, a few years back. Froze my ass off looking forward to my JD shot, but at the end of our distillery tour, a nice lady brought out samples of...lemonade! *Gee, thanks.*

And in other countries...

If you're ever in Amsterdam, you'll see a hook at the top of the houses that stand along the canal. Most people wonder what it's for. It's so the Dutch can get their furniture into their house. Most places along the canals do not have elevators, and the stairs are too narrow. I have had the pleasure (not) of having to wait in a line of traffic until a piano was hoisted up and into a home. Canal streets are too small to pass in a car, though on a bike you're okay.

You are also not allowed to bring more than two packs of chewing gum into Singapore. If you bring more than two, you could face a $5,000 fine for gum smuggling and one year in jail. If you are caught leaving your chewed gum on the ground or any other place, you could be beaten with a bamboo stick! Ouch.

It's illegal to wear high heels to the Acropolis in Greece. I personally couldn't even imagine walking around the ruins in a pair of stilettos, but I suppose it has happened.

It's illegal to hike naked in Switzerland. Yep, the Swiss banned naked hiking. *Well, there goes my trip! Switzerland just doesn't sound like fun anymore.*

LOOK AT WHAT'S IN YOUR OWN BACKYARD

Hanging with the locals in the Everglades.

When it comes to travel, sometimes all we need to do is look in our own backyard.

When we grow up in a certain area of the world, we take for granted some of the amazing and historical places that our own area has to offer. I have heard it many times before: "Oh, I can see that anytime," or, "I'll go another day."

Years ago when I was in Paris, I met a guy who had lived there his entire life. When I started to ask him questions about the Eiffel Tower, he said, "You know, I have never been in the Eiffel Tower." *What? I thought every French person in Paris had been to the Eiffel Tower.* He said, "I never really had a reason to go inside." Yet almost every day, he passed it on his way to work. I can only imagine that after a while you just forget it's even there, because you take for granted it always will be.

I suppose it's the same with people who have lived their

entire life in New York City but have never gone to the Empire State Building or out to Ellis Island to see the Statue of Liberty.

When I was in Norway for a month, I said to my Norwegian friend Arne, "Let's drive to Sweden." It's about 200 miles to the Swedish border, but it turned out he'd never been. I said, "Let's do it!" I was young and wanted to be able to say I'd gone to Sweden. So we did, and he enjoyed the trip.

I, too, am guilty of taking places for granted. Growing up in central Pennsylvania, it was only a two-hour drive to Philadelphia, but I have never seen the Liberty Bell or the Philadelphia Museum of Art, with those famous steps that Sylvester Stallone ran up in the movie *Rocky*.

I have, however, visited places like Hershey, Lancaster's Amish country, and the Poconos, once a famous honeymoon spot and known for its champagne-glass bathtubs and heart-shaped beds.

We tend to forget about famous places or tourist traps when we live close to them. Maybe we think we can see that monument or visit that town anytime, but we never actually take the time to go.

I've been like that when it comes to visiting certain states. For something to really pique my interest, I feel the need to travel much farther away than just a short plane ride. I know I should really think about changing that habit. Maybe I will break down and go visit the Grand Canyon one of these days. It's close, and in all my years, I have never been.

Key West is a good example of a popular travel destination. You hear about it all the time, and it's especially popular with cruise lines. However, I know so many people who live in South Florida and have yet to make the drive or take a short plane or boat ride to the Keys. They go as far as Key Largo or Islamorada but don't make the entire trip to Key West, which is only three and a half hours from Miami.

Living most of my life in California, I have taken advantage of some of what the West Coast has to offer—places like Wine Country in Napa Valley, with all its beautiful views and landscapes that go along with the wineries. It's even lovelier if you are lucky enough to catch all the hot air balloons floating in the sky. That area reminds me of the South of France. But I still haven't really put a dent in it.

Carmel-by-the-Sea is a quaint little town that's always nice to visit. And of course the original Disneyland is an option. There are places along the coast like Big Sur and Hearst Castle, and I'll never forget the little town we came across while driving down the coast years ago: the sign said, "Harmony, population seventeen." I wonder if that's still true.

You never know what you might come across when you explore a little more.

If you like skiing in the winter or hiking in the summer, then Mt. High and Mt. Baldy are just a short trip away from Los Angeles. California is one of the few places where you can enjoy the beach and then drive an hour and a half and be on a ski slope—the best of both worlds, all in one day. You can do the same in Santiago, Chile.

And if you happen to live in the state of Kentucky, please at some point in your life make your way to the Kentucky Derby. Even if you're not into horse racing, you will still enjoy it. It's fun and fabulous, and the fashion is outrageous. I could sit all day watching the colorful outfits worn by both men and women. The hats are to die for! Some are hysterically funny, while others gorgeous—and the bigger, the better. As they say, it really is the most exciting two minutes in sports.

What I can say is if you live in a place that's famous for

something, venture out to see it. *Why not?* You might surprise yourself. If, in the end, you aren't impressed, then at least you can say, "Been there, done that!"

All we really have to do is open our eyes and look around us. There is always something new to explore, a place we may have forgotten about or perhaps didn't have much interest in visiting.

Rethink it...these places may not always be there for us.

What we take for granted today, people pay to visit and explore.

So don't wait! Life is meant to be lived!

TRAVELING SOLO

I'm not sure what the big deal is with a woman sitting at a bar enjoying a glass of wine on her own—or even having dinner by herself. I suppose there's an old stigma attached to it that says this woman is alone because she is looking for company or waiting to be approached. Personally, I enjoy my alone time, and on many occasions I have gone out to dinner by myself—a.k.a. "loser party of one," but *I love it.* I definitely do not want to be approached or offered a drink by anyone. I just simply want to sit and enjoy whatever it is I'm drinking or eating and do some people-watching.

On numerous occasions, I have actually been approached by men who thought I was some kind of working girl. *Really?* Once I was in a very lovely wine and cheese cellar in Vegas, enjoying a tasting, when a man came up to me and asked if I would like to join him upstairs. *What?* I've also been asked if I would like some company while sitting in the dining area of a Las Vegas bar. *Company...no.*

If you're a single woman and you're dressed up halfway decent, what gives a man the right to automatically assume you're a working girl? Another time, I stepped out of the ladies' room on my way back to a gambling table to join my boyfriend at the time. About five pit workers walked by—both men and women—looked at me, looked at each other, and said, "Hey, there goes a working girl!" I was wearing a black suit with a skirt, jacket, and turtleneck, so why did they assume I was a working girl?

I have traveled solo throughout my life, whether it was for work, on a job, on a holiday—whatever. I just enjoy being on my own. I am a loner, and I am my own best friend. People find it weird or odd, and they always say, "I can't believe you did that or went there on your own!" To which I reply, "What do you want me to do, wait for someone to take me or ask me?" Heck no, time is short!

You have to see and do things while you're able and healthy enough. I have known so many people who said, "I'm going to go visit this place or that place once I retire," and then once they retired, they fell ill, were too tired, or even passed away.

Remember: time is short.

There was a song recorded by Three Dog Night called "One." You would remember it if you heard it. They sing about one being the loneliest number, but I don't think one is a lonely number at all. I think one is fabulous.

One...allows you to enjoy peace and quiet.

One...allows you to go shopping on your own without having to hurry in the dressing room because someone is waiting for you.

One...allows you to wake up and make the coffee just how you like it!

And one is solo, me, myself, and I—my own best friend.

I have lived with men for probably half my life. Some of those relationships lasted longer than others, but at this stage in my life, I prefer to be alone. Men are there if I need them, but I don't need one in my house permanently!

I enjoy my freedom and my alone time, with no one to put a wrinkle in my couch or a water glass on the sink. I enjoy all of that. Some of you would think it's very odd, maybe even selfish, but choosing freedom and choosing to live my life how I want to live it isn't selfish. It's my choice, and everyone deserves to live life how they wish.

Life is meant to be lived, and I want to enjoy!

MORE SPIRITS AND SUPERSTITIONS

I definitely believe there is some sort of afterlife, and I'm hoping it's as peaceful, serene, and calm as some of the stories I've heard and read about near-death experiences.

Over the years, and especially when my father was ill, I read many books on death and dying. I wanted to know what to expect at the end of someone's life. I discovered a whole other world of stories from people—both kids and adults—who have had near-death experiences.

They described how their spirit hovered above their body, watching everything that was happening to and around them. Then for one reason or another, the spirit was placed back inside the body. They could describe exactly what happened to them and how they felt at the time. Most say the same thing: calm, peace, joy.

I have a girlfriend who was diagnosed with cancer, completely out of the blue. I asked her if it was okay for me to share what she had experienced, and she gave me her permission, thanking me for not thinking she was crazy.

She was athletic, fit, and a picture of health, until one day, her life changed in an instant.

Not only did she have cancer, she had a very rare form of it. It's shocking to think someone is fine and then, in the blink of an eye, lying on their deathbed like she was.

After her almost two-year battle through hell, she told me what she had experienced.

During one of her hospital stays, when I can only imagine the pain she must have been feeling, all of a sudden her family members who had passed on were with her. She said she couldn't quite see them clearly, as if there was a veil separating her from them. At the time, she thought, "There is no way this is happening. This is a dream. Forget this—I'm out of here!"

A few weeks later, when she was once again back in the hospital, this time for a bone marrow transplant, they were with her again. Her father, grandmother, and all of her uncles who had passed on from cancer, sat there on chairs as if they had been waiting for her. She said once again, there was a veil between them, but this time she was able to pass through the veil. She told me they spoke to her and told her she had to go back because she had more to do. She begged and begged them to please let her stay with them. It was so peaceful and calm that she didn't want to leave. She said there was no white light or anything like that, just pure peace. But once again they said, "You have to go back."

I asked her, "Were you in a room? What was it like?" It was hard for her to explain, but she said it was as if she was feeling their presence in front of her and they were communicating with her. She named everyone who was with her during that time. She wanted so badly to stay with them, and to this day, she isn't sure why she was sent back. She feels there must be a reason. I told her she will figure it out one day. She no longer has a fear of dying because she knows it's peaceful and loved ones are waiting for her when her time comes.

When my dad became sick, he was in and out of the hospital for two years. Almost every month, I would get a call that he was back in the hospital, and I'd fly home from California. I did this up until the end, when I stayed home for what would be his last two months.

During those last two months, he was in and out of consciousness, but mostly out. It's surprising what people hear when you think they are totally out of it. I knew from reading books that although someone may be unconscious, they can still hear what's going on around them. This was true of my dad. He was in an area of the hospital where they send patients when there isn't anything more to do for them—or as my dad called it, "the last stop before the basement." He still managed to make us laugh.

One morning when I walked into his room during one of his episodes of being in and out of consciousness, he said, "The lady across the hall died last night." I asked how he knew, and he said, "I heard them zipping up the bag." *Jeez, really dad?* You wonder how much someone hears while out of it and why they hear certain things and not others, and I don't even know how he knew it was a lady.

My siblings and I wanted to bring him home, so we took him back to his house and set everything up to make him as comfortable as possible. For almost two months, this man was out of it and unresponsive except to tell us about the dying lady across the hall. But on the day we brought him home and put him in his room, he sat straight up in bed, looked at us and said, "I want a hot dog!"

I said, "Really?"

"Yep," he said, "and I want it from the Hot Dog King!"

So off I went in search of his hot dog! He wasn't awake for very long, and during that time, he talked about how he saw his dad. Then he said, "Dorothy was here, but she couldn't stay." Dorothy was my mother. All I could think was that she came to bring him with her, but perhaps he wasn't quite ready.

The family took turns sleeping in my dad's room with him during this time. We all stayed within a few steps of him. I was in his room the night he passed. I watched as he threw off his covers, put his arms in the air as if he was leaving his body, and with his leg, he took one giant step. I called for the rest of the family, and he said, "I gotta get out of here." Not long after, he did just that. He was gone.

Later, I walked into the living room, and as I waited for the representative from the funeral home to arrive, the biggest moth I have ever seen in my life appeared on the wall. I'm talking bomber-style aircraft moth out of nowhere. This is Pennsylvania! In all my years of growing up there, never have I ever seen such a thing!

I said to my sisters, "Look, it's dad!" At first they thought I was nuts, but since that day, we have all seen some sort of moth whenever it's a birthday or if we've been thinking or talking about him. I can even remember driving through the streets of LA one day, thinking about my dad. When I stopped at a red light, what do you think was sitting nice and cozy on the car bumper in front of me? You guessed it—*my dad!*

When I was searching for a property in South Florida, I had a real estate agent from Denmark who was well into her eighties. She would drive me around, and we would pull up in front of a house I was supposed to be looking at. Sometimes I would go in, and sometimes I wouldn't. She would look at me and say in her Danish accent, "But why do you not want to go in and see this house?" And I would say, "No, thank you, it's a ghost house." She just looked at me like I was nuts. This happened a few times, and she finally said, "You people from LA are crazy!"

It's like when I went to that old farmhouse on the Camino and knew in advance there would be something there just by looking at the photos. From the minute I stepped in the door, I felt it. When I walk into a place and get a bad or strange feeling, I think twice about staying there.

Something else I am highly superstitious about is writing a will. I know it isn't a very smart thing, but I just can't help it. I feel like if you're writing a last will and testament, *then that's it for you.* It's as if I might jinx myself. I know one of these days I'm going to have to bite the bullet and just do it, but then again, I say that every year.

I have heard all the stories about people dying right after they wrote a will or when getting ready to write one: "Oh, the poor guy just finished his will," or, "She was just saying the other day how she needs to write a will." And so I continue to put it off. Maybe after this, I will come to my senses.

Taking someone's phone number and personal information out of my phone after they pass away is something I can never bring myself to do. I still have friends' info in my phone although they have been gone for years. I'm not sure why—maybe just to remind me once in a while that they existed.

One was a longtime friend in LA and also my pet sitter for twenty-plus years. She passed away at such a young age—in her late thirties. The odd thing is, it's not so much her phone number that stood out as it was her email address that I will never forget. It was Livealytl, as in "live a little," which is exactly what she did—she lived just a little because she died so young. I try not to use that phrase very often. *I want to live more than just a little!*

As I was writing this chapter, I was visiting family in Pennsylvania. We got together for the first time in a long time with both my sisters and my brother, so we decided to take a group photo. Later, I noticed a gigantic orb in the picture, bigger than I have ever seen. I've seen much smaller ones before, but *this one was huge.* At the very top was something that looked like a small rainbow. The orb started high above my head and went straight down across my face and body, ending up in a slant that also touched the feet of my older sister. Is someone watching over me, or watching all of us? I think so. My siblings think I'm a bit nuts, but the orb made them reconsider.

Thank you, Angels!

PART VII

38

So You Know…

THESE DAYS, I REALLY DON'T THINK TOO MUCH ABOUT HOW much longer I will live—it was mostly a thirty-eight thing. Now being sixty, what do I have left—another twenty years? We don't have a crystal ball to let us know when our time is up, and that's probably a good thing.

I don't like to dwell too much on illness or aches and pains. I just had a conversation with a girlfriend yesterday about people our age who only want to talk about their ailments, and for some reason, they feel the need to tell you in detail.

Please! I'm old enough, and I don't need to feel any older! I don't want to hear everyone's issues. Let's talk positive, people. It's depressing, so please don't tell me about all your personal illness issues unless I ask you, and chances are, I won't. Sorry if that sounds brutal, but I'm just being honest.

Speaking of being honest, writing this book has been the best therapy ever! Remembering everything, getting it out of my mind, and seeing it on paper has been so therapeutic. Of course, some parts were harder than others to write about (like

what you're about to read), but once I got it out, it was done—
end of story!

IN THE BEGINNING

My mom.

I was born in Pennsylvania in the Harrisburg hospital on February 10, 1962, and raised just outside Harrisburg in a small town. My childhood was typical, or at least I thought so until I decided to write this book.

Looking back now, I suppose some might say I had a tragic childhood. But for me, it was just my life. If you don't know any other way, then that's how it is. I had a sister who was five years older than me and a brother who was ten years older. Within the first six years of my life, whatever path I was born to follow took a sharp turn in another direction.

Late at night on February 9, 1968, the week of my sixth birthday, I heard my father calling out to my brother, who was almost sixteen. He was asking for him to come help because he found my mother lying on the floor in the bathroom. She was on her back, looking into the ceiling light above, but couldn't see anything and was very confused. She was also eight months pregnant.

They got her up off the floor, put her in bed, and called an ambulance. My sister, with pink hair rollers in her hair, and I sat quietly on the steps, watching as the EMTs strapped our mother onto the gurney and rolled her away.

During the week my mother was in the hospital, my sixth birthday party was to take place. We were to celebrate it on February 10. I remember all the mothers coming to the door to drop the kids off and quietly whispering with my Aunt Ruth about how Dorothy (my mother) was doing. I could see Aunt Ruth nodding her head as if something was wrong, but all I really understood was it was my birthday, and I was going to eat cake and ice cream and open presents. I really don't remember much else.

The following day, February 11, was my mother's birthday. We were still waiting for word on her condition. I suppose everyone already knew the outcome, and I don't think in 1968 they would have allowed us kids to visit in the hospital anyway. One morning, a few days later, I heard the phone ring and watched as my dad sat on the edge of his bed, the old dial telephone in his hand. I knew the doctor was talking to him. Then I heard him say, "Okay, thank you." As he hung up, tears rolled down his face. I didn't say anything, but somehow even at that age, I just knew that my mother wouldn't be coming home.

My mother was eight months pregnant and had not been feeling well. She apparently went to the doctor, who ran a few tests and told her if there was a problem, the office would contact her. In other words, "don't call us—we'll call you."

That weekend, we went to her parents' house a few hours away. She still wasn't feeling well, so we came home early. Later that night is when my dad found her on the floor. She was in a state of confusion. She passed away from something called toxemia of pregnancy or preeclampsia, which apparently is common. In this day and age, if it's caught in time, you usually don't die. Both my mother and the baby died.

I can't recall anything about my life with her prior to that week in February.

I do remember the funeral. Looking back now, I can say I was glad that they allowed me to go. It seems like there was a time when parents thought it would be too stressful for a child to attend a funeral at such a young age. They wanted to keep children away from tragic events. But seeing her lying in her coffin at the viewing and again at the church, and watching the casket being taken to the cemetery, gave me closure.

I remember my dad holding me as I looked down at her sleeping peacefully. He asked if I wanted to kiss my mom goodbye, and I shook my head no. He said, "Are you sure?" *Yes.* Again, I shook my head. I must have understood, even at that young age, that although it was my mom's body lying in front of me, her spirit was no longer with her.

My Aunt Lucille told me years later that she couldn't be there for the funeral (she was living in Greece at the time), but she heard at the viewing I was twirling in my daisy dress and kept saying, "See my new dress? Do you like my new dress?" *Oh, how I wish I had that dress today.*

My Aunt Lucille told me that they were afraid to tell my Aunt Lorraine that my mom had passed away, because she too was pregnant and about ready to deliver. Before Lorraine learned of my mother's death, she had an experience she shared with us. She said she was lying down in the afternoon, taking a nap, and saw Mom in a dream. Mom was walking up a staircase, wearing a long white dress. As she reached the top, she turned around and waved to Lorraine. I guess it was my mom's way of saying goodbye to her sister.

Later at home, one of my grandmothers asked me, "Do you understand that your mom's not coming back?" I nodded my head. Yes, I understood. Looking back, had I not been allowed to attend the viewing and the funeral, I would have always been thinking she was out there somewhere and might walk through the door again. I would have expected to appear on one of those famous talk shows in the '90s and then, "Surprise—here's your mom!" But I saw she was gone with my own eyes, and even at six, I understood it was final.

Most of my life, I have said her death did not affect me like it affected my older siblings. I believe that because of their ages, eleven and fifteen, it was much harder on them. My sister was overly protective of my nieces when they were growing up, to the point that it probably made them crazy. I don't think they could grasp that it was because of losing our mother so young. My brother, on the other hand, seemed to have a lot of anger, which sometimes was directed at his kids, my nephews.

And then there was me. I never had kids and had no desire

to. I think subconsciously I thought, *If I get pregnant, I will die.* I'm also not like everyone else who sees a pregnant woman and thinks it's beautiful. I'm sorry, I just don't, and I know it's because of my childhood experience. To me, it relates to something painful, both physically and mentally.

Only later in life did I see how much her death affected me.

When asked if I remember my mom, it's always the same answer, the same scenario, the same story like a broken record that plays over and over again in my head. *The last week only: her on the floor, our birthday week, that phone call on Valentine's Day that must have broken my dad's heart, the funeral, and being asked if I understood.*

In our family, we didn't discuss it. I never had therapy, although I'm sure I could have used a lot of it. Remember, it was 1968, and you didn't talk about certain things in those days, especially traumatic events. I thought it was just my family, but after researching and listening to other stories, it seems as if it was not uncommon to let life move forward without processing—to block pain out of memory, which is exactly what I did for almost fifty-three years.

My sister reminds me every year, the same week, "Can you believe it's been X number of years?"

"Yes," I say, "long time," and then we move on to another subject. There's a part of me that wants to talk, but another part of me feels uncomfortable talking about something we never discussed in the early years.

I continued on without my mother and with my dad as my primary parent. He did everything for the next four years, until he married my stepmother. As a child, you don't think much about what your parents do for you or how they must have been grieving, but as an adult, I think about it much more.

I never again saw my maternal grandparents or my mother's

siblings, except for one sister. It was as if they just vanished. Families are strange, but I couldn't imagine tossing away my nieces or nephews just because I no longer had my sister or brother. It's even weirder to me to stop having a relationship with your grandkids.

When I think about my mother, I think about all the events that she never lived long enough to see. Googling the year 1968, I found out it was the most tumultuous year in history—for our family, but also for the country. There were the shocking assassinations of MLK and JFK. Apollo 8 orbited space. There was a much hated war, and Nixon won the White House. Then she missed everything in the decades after that—she didn't see the evolution of automobiles or computers, cordless telephones, push-button telephones, any kind of cell phone. I mean, imagine FaceTime back then—it was something you would only see on a cartoon like *The Jetsons*.

Then there are all the personal and private events, like all of our high school graduations, weddings, children being born, holidays, birthdays, and other good times when having your mother is very important.

That's what's hard to wrap my head around: someone has been gone for so long, missed so much, and still, the world has advanced in many ways.

38

During lockdown, I was always dreaming about my next travel adventure. Then I realized that most of my experiences were crammed into a span of thirty-eight years. It got me wondering why. *Why have I always felt the need to see and do as much as I can in high gear?*

There was only one answer.

Life is meant to be lived! Saint-Émilion, France.

It was because I had always felt that my time was short on this Earth. I was convinced I would be dead by the age of thirty-eight. After all, that's the age my mother was when she passed. Growing older than your own mother was when she died? *Strange*. Having wrinkles when your mother did not, because she didn't live long enough to get them? *Also weird.*

I could never imagine living past thirty-eight.

So for many years, I lived my life in fast-forward, subconsciously thinking, *I have to see the world—it has so much to offer!* It's a cliché, but all you ever hear is how life is short. Now, I prefer to say *time is short.*

There was a time in my life when it felt like people all around me were dying. My mother, my grandmother, my booking agent, Irena—all the women I became close to in my life were moving on to the afterlife.

So I read books on death and dying, anything I could find on the subject. I especially loved the books by Elisabeth Kübler-Ross. She was a pioneer in near-death studies, and I found her work fascinating.

Then I became interested in mediums—the people who talk to the dead and deliver messages to you.

I was curious and I didn't want to be afraid when the time came...at thirty-eight. So I did what I could to prepare myself.

On my thirty-eighth birthday, I waited for it—*and I had to wait that entire year.*

Every time I threw my leg over a motorcycle, I recited to myself my ritual motorcycle prayer: *I promise not to ride faster than my angels can fly.*

I also said the airplane prayer in my seat, right before take off: *keep me safe on this flight all the way to my destination.*

And when I went to sleep at night, there was the bedtime prayer: *please just let me wake up in the morning.* It went on and on that year, and then magically I turned thirty-nine!

But I still waited. I thought for sure my number got mixed up with another person's. That's the only reason I am still here. Maybe God didn't recognize me with all my Botox.

I kept on moving, kept traveling, kept pushing forward in life. I wanted to do as much as possible. After all, I would say I have learned way more from traveling than I ever could have from sitting in a geography or history class.

It's only been since I reached my fifties that I have started to feel more relaxed, though now I have to think about old age setting in and how I cannot turn back the clock. I turned sixty while writing this book!

That means for the fifty-four years since my mother passed away, I have thought about how much longer I will live on pretty much a daily basis. But it has also pushed me to enjoy my life to the fullest, with every bone in my body.

When people told me I'd have to slow down one day and stay in one place, I wondered, *what for?* No one could ever give me a good answer. It wasn't like I had kids to worry about. I was free to go.

I stayed silent about my past for most of my life. Fifty-four years is a long time to stay silent. I only offered info about my mother's death when asked, and I wasn't asked too many times in my life.

While walking the Camino in 2019, my friend and I talked about a lot of things. We walked thirteen miles a day for a week, so what else was there to do but talk and gossip? One day, out of the blue, she asked, "What happened to your mother?"

I had known her for more than thirty years, and she never knew my story. So I told her.

At this age, I find myself thinking more about my mom and of the silence that stayed within the walls of my house growing up. All I can hope for is that someone reads this book and says, "I don't want to hold my silence for fifty-four years the way she did."

I didn't have an option back in 1968, and so many years went by afterward that it felt like it was just too late. But in reality, it's never too late for anything.

Writing this book has been therapeutic in many ways—letting it all out, reliving the past through my stories and travels, and especially speaking about my mother. The mother I never knew. The mother who became nothing more than a password in my computer, thinking that would somehow keep her alive, at least in my mind. The mother we never, ever talked about in my family, to the point that when her name did come up, it was painfully uncomfortable.

There is also a part of me that long wondered about the circumstances of her death and what exactly she died from. I'd never seen the death certificate; I only knew what I was told all those years ago. I needed to see for myself, so after fifty-four years, I ordered a copy of her death certificate just to put my mind at ease. It was easier than I thought.

The day it came in the mail, I left it on my table, afraid I might learn something sinister. Oh my, I allowed my imagination to run wild for a minute, and then I sat down and opened the envelope, finding nothing more than what I was told so many years ago. Cause of death: Toxemia of Pregnancy. There it was, written in black and white. Case closed.

Even at this age, I have not allowed myself to slow down. *You slow down, you die.* So I keep moving from the time I wake up in the morning until I rest my head at night. I stay on the move. It's as if I'm always hurrying.

I'm a firm believer that if something tragic happens in your life, you don't have to dwell on that event. You need to pick yourself up and move on. Take time to mourn, then keep going.

Strive to make it, and know that you deserve the best in life.

Maybe it's a way of covering up what happened to me in my young life, but it's how I deal.

And it worked for me. I'm content with all my experiences and all that I have accomplished in life.

If I had only one wish, I would ask for my mother to be here, even if only for a day. I would bombard her with questions that I do not and never will know the answers to. I'm pretty sure one of the reasons I never had kids was because I was always so worried I would die young and leave them without a mother—allowing history to repeat itself. I had to break the cycle, or so I thought. You always hear that phrase "things happen for a reason," but I'm not entirely sure I know the reason why my mother was taken from me so young.

Was it because if she stayed, I would never have done all of the things I did? Would I have been stuck in the little town where I grew up? Would I not have lived such a fabulous life in Europe or met my Dutchman? Would I still have moved to LA and worked for *Playboy*? Everything is one big question mark. Maybe she had to go so I could have a different life—who knows?

There were times when I wanted to ask my dad questions regarding my mom, but because we never talked about her in our house, I just couldn't bring myself to. Do I regret it? Not really. I don't think regrets have ever been an option for me. I live and learn, and I move forward thinking, *Maybe in my after-life I will get the answers to all those questions.*

One thing I know is that I cannot live my life beating myself up over unanswered questions.

My dad did the best he could, and I think he did a great job considering he was left to pick up the pieces and deal with three young children on his own until he remarried years later.

I'm sure there were men out there, especially in 1968, who would not have known what to do on their own with three kids. But he did everything for us, and I am thankful for that. How hard it must've been for him and how lonely. He not only lost my mother but an unborn child as well. I have really only thought about that later on in life, what my father must have been going through while taking care of three young kids all on his own. I can only imagine the pain and suffering he must have endured silently.

I'm curious who that unborn child was. Would I have had a younger sister? Or a brother? Everything that surrounds my mother is nothing but one big question mark! It's terrible, but I have to force myself to remember that I also lost a sibling. Because I was so young and don't even remember my mother or her pregnancy, it's hard to imagine that I lost a brother or a sister.

Everything that could have been, never happened. Your life changes forever when you least expect it, and you start to think about all the "what ifs." But then I remember if I'd had that sibling, I would not have had my little sister, who is the daughter of my stepmother. You can't keep going through life and saying, "what if," or you will drive yourself crazy.

This is the life I have always known. It's hard to imagine it any other way.

After my dad passed away in 1997, I had dreams about him. For a long time, it was like he was trying to come to me. But I have never in my life dreamed of my mother. I'm not sure if it's because I was too young or what the reason is, but I always wished for it.

For some reason, I feel that I'm always being protected by someone. I don't know why or who it is, but I feel it. Something or someone is looking over me. Several times I've even felt a tap on my left shoulder. It's weird, but it's as if someone stands behind me. Others might disagree, I choose to take it as a sign from someone.

Time is short. Don't dream your dreams—live them.

Life is meant to be lived.

CPSIA information can be obtained
at www.ICGtesting.com
Printed in the USA
LVHW031130050423
743446LV00001B/239